CAMBRIDGE LIBRARY COLLECTION

Books of enduring scholarly value

Women's Writing

The later twentieth century saw a huge wave of academic interest in women's writing, which led to the rediscovery of neglected works from a wide range of genres, periods and languages. Many books that were immensely popular and influential in their own day are now studied again, both for their own sake and for what they reveal about the social, political and cultural conditions of their time. A pioneering resource in this area is Orlando: Women's Writing in the British Isles from the Beginnings to the Present (http://orlando.cambridge.org), which provides entries on authors' lives and writing careers, contextual material, timelines, sets of internal links, and bibliographies. Its editors have made a major contribution to the selection of the works reissued in this series within the Cambridge Library Collection, which focuses on non-fiction publications by women on a wide range of subjects from astronomy to biography, music to political economy, and education to prison reform.

A Few Words to the Jews

Charlotte Montefiore (1818–54) published *A Few Words to the Jews* anonymously in 1853. The volume is a collection of nine essays on Anglo-Jewish life, covering topics including the Sabbath, Jewish women, religious reform and practice, Jewish materialism, immorality, the idea of truth, and religious festivals. The essays, like Montefiore's collection of didactic short stories, *The Cheap Jewish Library,* and her novel, *Caleb Asher*, carry a strong message of social justice. Montefiore, a wealthy, aristocratic and influential Jew, was deeply involved in social welfare and the education of young people within her community, establishing a number of foundations to aid underprivileged Jews, including the Jewish Emigration Society. In *A Few Words* Montefiore argued her case against social inequality and economic exploitation within Jewish communities. This is a rare example of nineteenth-century Anglo-Jewish writing, offering a fascinating insight into the social life and politics of Victorian Jews. For more information on this author, see http://orlando.cambridge.org/public/svPeople?person_id=montc2

Cambridge University Press has long been a pioneer in the reissuing of out-of-print titles from its own backlist, producing digital reprints of books that are still sought after by scholars and students but could not be reprinted economically using traditional technology. The Cambridge Library Collection extends this activity to a wider range of books which are still of importance to researchers and professionals, either for the source material they contain, or as landmarks in the history of their academic discipline.

Drawing from the world-renowned collections in the Cambridge University Library, and guided by the advice of experts in each subject area, Cambridge University Press is using state-of-the-art scanning machines in its own Printing House to capture the content of each book selected for inclusion. The files are processed to give a consistently clear, crisp image, and the books finished to the high quality standard for which the Press is recognised around the world. The latest print-on-demand technology ensures that the books will remain available indefinitely, and that orders for single or multiple copies can quickly be supplied.

The Cambridge Library Collection will bring back to life books of enduring scholarly value (including out-of-copyright works originally issued by other publishers) across a wide range of disciplines in the humanities and social sciences and in science and technology.

A Few Words
to the Jews

CHARLOTTE MONTEFIORE

CAMBRIDGE UNIVERSITY PRESS

Cambridge, New York, Melbourne, Madrid, Cape Town, Singapore,
São Paolo, Delhi, Dubai, Tokyo, Mexico City

Published in the United States of America by Cambridge University Press, New York

www.cambridge.org
Information on this title: www.cambridge.org/9781108020367

© in this compilation Cambridge University Press 2010

This edition first published 1853
This digitally printed version 2010

ISBN 978-1-108-02036-7 Paperback

A FEW WORDS

TO

THE JEWS.

BY

ONE OF THEMSELVES.

LONDON:

PUBLISHED FOR THE AUTHOR, BY

JOHN CHAPMAN, 142, STRAND.

MDCCCLIII.

A FEW WORDS

TO

THE JEWS.

BY

ONE OF THEMSELVES.

LONDON:

PUBLISHED FOR THE AUTHOR, BY

JOHN CHAPMAN, 142, STRAND.

MDCCCLIII.

London: Printed by Woodfall and Kinder.
Angel Court, Skinner Street.

CONTENTS.

A FEW WORDS

THE JEWS.

CHAPTER I.

THE PRESENT AGE AND JUDAISM.

THIS is a wonder-teeming age, very great and very glorious. Science and art take giant strides. Improvements and discoveries are brought forth in such quick succession that yesterday's marvel is consigned to oblivion by to-day's more wonderful exploit, or rare invention, or work of surpassing interest.

The world was once borne down a slow and turbid stream; it passed along like a huge barge upon a stagnant river; but now it is carried forward upon a resistless tide, and with full-spread sail it meets the wind and wave and surge. We leave the ancient landmarks far behind us, and for this new era time must invent some new method of chronicling its annals, for the old

B

ones are not sufficient guides as to the novelty
and antiquity of our works.   The Crystal Palace
that rose into life and beauty, as by a magi-
cian's wand, and disappeared like a phantom,
was a symbol of the age.   It contained within
its precincts the works of science, art, and humanity, that are the glory of the age.   The vast
edifice, its long aisles, its crowded galleries, were
hung with the trophies won by genius and industry, won in hard-fought battles by the vete-
rans whose hair had grown gray and bodies
feeble in the service of their liege masters; and
there, in proud array, those trophies rose one
above another, and, glittering in the sun of a
bright May morning, they smiled a welcome on
each passer-by, on peasant, peer, and prince.

There lay the harvest of the noblest conquest
of all time, the fruit of a victory not gained over
helpless human creatures, over fallen nations, over
an enslaved people; but of mind over matter—
of genius, of labour, and of patience over the
despotism of poverty, over the intolerance and
the ignorance of society.   No wail of misery, no
widowed or orphaned anguish, no clamours of
a pining liberty, no execrations of a chained
despair, mingled with the triumph.   This victory
was solemnized by all nations, was saluted by

a universal rejoicing, was consecrated by prayer, and was dedicated to the Supreme Being.

From this vast storehouse of perfected labour the mind travels to scenes of active industry. It explores the manufactory, investigates the ponderous locomotive, examines the delicate and skilful machinery, surveys the busy hands turning the wheel, weaving bright textures at the loom, and hammering at the iron forge. It penetrates into the sanctuaries of science and genius, seeks the chemist's laboratory, the poet's hearth, the artist's studio; and everywhere, alike in the stirring presence of commerce, in factory, mill, and dock, and in the quiet home of thought where mind labours in solitude and in silence, we meet with teeming heads and hearts, that are giving birth to new enterprises, new ideas, and new discoveries, that shall make earth more beautiful, the world more true and holy, and man greater and wiser.

The creative genius of a few gifted minds and the industry and toil of the many are not, however, the chief characteristics of the age; they lie most especially in the moral and intellectual progress of the mass. Education is no longer confined, like entailed estates or funded property, to the upper and wealthy classes; it is no longer

the exclusive possession of a caste; is no longer
inclosed in collegiate walls, in the seminaries of
rich men's sons, in the libraries of noble mansions; but it works its way amidst the people,
and penetrates into dark alleys and humble
homes. It is the good genius of many a lowly
hearth. Schools, clubs, mechanics' institutes,
libraries for the working classes, are rising up
in every city and district, and the indigent stu-
dent, the poor artist, the intellectual labourer
have found, at last, an oasis in the desert of their
lives—a fountain of sweet waters amid the arid
wastes and parched ground around them. Who
shall say what new stores of happiness, what
widened sphere of thought, is thus opened to
many an aspiring mind? Who shall say, through
this timely help, how many an impulse is developed into action, how many an embryo conception is quickened into life? A blessing on the
age which, amidst its profuse expenditure, amidst
its pomps and its shows, has not forgotten the
wants of a common humanity; but watches over
and assists the moral and mental development of
the mass! It is a happy thing for England this
education of her people, for from amidst her
people her ranks of greatness must be filled.
Their moral strength and intelligence must reno-

vate their country's vigour; they are like the tri-
butary streams which, small in themselves, yet feed
the wide and noble river; and as these gush forth
with an impetuous power from the bare mountain side and jagged rock, so do the people's
energies spring from a rough and uncultivated
nature, but are pregnant with a vitality unknown
to the more polished and luxurious class.

This energy has to be directed, for, if left to its
own untutored guidance, it may stray into a
wrong channel or overstep the boundaries of pru-
dence, and then would devastate, instead of en-
riching, the land.

There is another happy tendency in this age,
which is, the growing sympathy between rich and
poor. They are still, indeed, too widely separated
by distinct interests, by the artificial convention-
alities of society, by abysses over which neither extreme ignorance nor pride can pass.   But
still many a connecting bridge has been built
between the two classes.

The claims of a common brotherhood are beginning to be felt; the soft hand of refinement,
and the rough one of labour, sometimes now
meet in a grasp of fellowship, and words, not
all pity on one side, or submission and subservience on the other, but of respect and sympathy

upon both, are now interchanged. Society has begun to feel, at last, that humanity, though it wears many aspects, is essentially the same in all places ; that all human hearts from the cradle to the grave beat with the same joys and griefs, the same hopes and fears, no matter whether the cradle has been rocked by poverty or guarded by wealth ; no matter whether the grave be found beneath cathedral dome and sculptured monument, or under the green sod of a village cemetery. The child reared in palace or in hut—the youth studying in college halls or ragged schools —the man amidst his worldly greatness or in his laborious and indigent life, have alike experienced the deepest emotions that human nature is susceptible of. Both reposed in the innocence of childhood upon a mother's breast, both had their first tears wiped away by a mother's lips, both in twilight's dreamy hours have listened to the tale or hymn or words of solemn tenderness breathed by a mother's voice, and to both this mighty affection that sheltered them from evil, and wrapped them in a close embrace, remains a hallowed memory, never wholly obliterated, never wholly lost, but, like a star that is seen now through and now over the shifting clouds of a stormy sky, it shines now athwart and now above the darkest mo-

ments of their lives. Both have felt, and both remember as an era in their lives, the awakening of
their intellect, the dawn of thought, the birthday of the soul, and both have sought in solitude
and freedom to give vent to the new aspirations
and new yearnings that were struggling for utterance and seeking for a wider development.

Both have felt the rapture of a first love, the
thrilling emotion of another human heart beating in unison against their own, and both have
then felt that the world had nothing more to
give or nothing to take away if it but allowed
these two hearts to remain thus for ever bound
in perfect harmony, love, and truth.

Both have watched beside the loved and dying,
both have wept tears of a choking grief above
the grave of a buried happiness and buried hope.
Both have struggled with temptation, battled
with sin, wrestled with despair ; both, in moments
of moral anguish or of moral victory, have looked
up into the same sky and called aloud upon
the same Almighty Being, the " Father of the
spirits of all flesh."

Oh, human hearts, does not the resemblance
of your inner life outweigh the discrepancies of
your outer existence !

The memories that twine around your heart
like perfumed flowers round the tree's rugged
stem, the aspirations that make your soul tremble
within you and beat against its prison bars, as
the bird longing for freedom flaps its wings
against its cage, the unutterable joy of requited
affection, the strife of passion with duty, the
weariness of conflict, the hope of repentance that
sheds its light upon the mind solemn and beautiful as the moon's calm beams shining upon the
dim aisles of a darkened but still holy sanctuary,
—these, these make up your lives, not your luxuries, not your wants, not your gold and silver,
not your indigence, not your sumptuous attire,
not your worn garments. Oh, human hearts,
you are indeed bound together by indissoluble
ties, by a kindredship of mind, and it is time for
one mighty throb of universal love to beat in the
bosom of mankind.

There is a glimmering light, the light of a true
brotherhood rising from out the clouds of a long
dark night. It gilds to-day the mountain top,
but by degrees it will surely spread further and
further until it illumines the whole earth. Thank
God, that we, in our day, have seen its dawn.

In this age of progress, and change, and assimilation, there is yet one people in England who stand somewhat in an isolated position, and whose sphere of action is restricted.

There is a wall of separation between the Jew and Christian which resists the innovations of the present day. Let it be understood it is not meant by this that there is a partition-wall betwixt the mind of Jew and Christian; these may fraternize together, exchange sympathies and friendships: it is of the worldly life we speak, the life of labour, of enterprise, of distinction, and of fame. Some barriers, built by intolerance and guarded by fanaticism and prejudice, still exist; and besides these there are some on our side over which the Jew cannot pass. A faithful adherence to his father's creed necessarily restricts the Jew's vocations, and closes many a path against him which smiles an alluring invitation.

He has (for who has not, who owns a country and a home?) patriotism, enthusiasm, and ambition; but these are fettered, or at least must find another scope for their gratification than in the careers that usually afford both the incentive and the reward. He may aspire after military and naval fame; he may delight in an adventurous career; or he may long for an agricultural life, for the country's bright skies, and vernal voice, and peaceful scenes; but the longing and the desire are subdued, for to cherish or to yield to either is to renounce a prouder ambition and a purer satisfaction, that of remaining true to the faith of Sinai, and sharing the destiny and enjoying the fellowship of those who hold a kindred name, a kindred worship, and a kindred hope.

Upon England's stately men-of-war, as they sail along the calm seas or gallantly battle with the rising gale and heaving waves, a brave crew offer up, night and morning, prayer and supplications to the God who rules the sea and storm. A day of rest is solemnized upon the wide ocean, and the Sabbaths celebrated on the deep seas, and the prayers that blend together above the voice of the waves, make the hardy sailor a yet braver man, fit him for his perilous life, nerve his heart and mind to face undauntedly danger and death. The Jew could not join in these religious rites, and his own religion would be desecrated or neglected. He cannot, then, as he dreams at night, take a place among that gallant crew, or wave upon the white-sprayed foaming sea his country's flag, or plant her standard upon a conquered shore.

In England's far-off isles, in her proud Indian domains, there are churches that recall by the most solemn of remembrances the national creed and the mother country to her self-exiled sons. There are priests who minister the first and last rites of religion; there are teachers and missionaries, who, amidst parched plains, or in rude homes, or amidst the sensuality of camps and the enervation of luxurious cities, endeavour to keep alive the religious sentiment within the soldier and the pilgrim's mind.

The Jew would be deprived of these safeguards and incentives to virtue; and though God may be worshipped, and most truly, where there is neither temple nor altar nor outward form, though we need no priest or rabbi to stand by our side when we approach the Almighty Father, though our conscience and our reason may speak to us holier words than teacher or missionary ever spoke, yet few of us have minds and hearts pure and strong and true enough to dispense with outward help. The early sanctuary, the time-honoured associations, the house of prayer, the solemn festival, the example of the many, the preacher's warning and solace,—these are yet needed to preserve us safe amidst the warfare and temptations of the world. The distant home

in India to which an honourable ambition calls so
many is no home for us.

Far away from the turmoil, smoke, and fog of
cities ; far away from the parched breath of fever
which invades crowded haunts, and infects with
a subtle poison narrow alleys and dark courts
and ill-ventilated dens ; far away from these polluted spots, amidst green fields and open meadows, amidst nature's smiles, the agriculturist
ploughs his land, sows his wheat, and reaps his
harvest.   Within a little space are gathered what
to him constitutes the wealth of *his* world.   His
cottage home peeps through the tall trees that
wave their green branches round it, and on his
return from his daily toil, as the setting sun
lights up with a living radiance the humble
dwelling, it smiles a bright welcome upon him.
Almost close by is his children's school, of which
the village is as proud as Oxford of its university, and all the week long blithesome voices
sound from out it—and the labourer pauses at
its wooden gate to single out from amidst the
many his children's voice, and then pursues
more cheerily his onward way, humming the
hymn just heard.   Above the cottage trees, and
visible from its casement, rises the church spire,
and softly and sweetly mingling with the breath

of early morning peals the Sabbath chime.   The meadow paths, the shady lane, are thronged with a peaceful multitude; labourers with their clean smock-frocks, matrons with white kerchiefs and hooded cloaks, and children with sparkling eyes, and rosy cheeks, and sturdy limbs, bend their steps to the house of prayer.   And there, wives and husbands, brothers and sisters, friends and comrades, together listen to the pastor's voice, the familiar voice which taught them when they yet were children, and there together they pray, where their fathers, who now sleep beneath the yews of the old churchyard, prayed before them. All their own, their living and their dead, are round them.   In his secluded village the Christian finds the hallowing influences, the tender memories, the friendships and companionships, that his moral and spiritual nature require for his noblest culture and highest development.

Now if a few Jews were to choose an agricultural life, they would necessarily, as things now stand, be cut off from much that is dear and sacred to them.   They would at once be deprived of their house of worship, of their children's school, of their early companions, of their aged parents, of the graves of the loved and departed, and these constitute life's holiest teachers and noblest enjoyments. They would lack the ministry, the sympathies, the recollections, the motives for self-denial and self-abnegation, without which the spiritual being grows very poor and very lonely. Neither blue skies nor fragrant air could compensate for their loss. Our physical nature might grow hardier beneath fresher air and blithesome sunshine, but our moral life would be deprived of its most invigorating elements, and it would surely dwindle into weakness and insignificance. Many have felt this, though perhaps not defined their feelings clearly or expressed in words what England's greatest living poetess has so beautifully said :—

> " I will have hopes that cannot fade,
>   For flowers the valley yields ;
> I will have humble thoughts instead
>   Of silent dewy fields.
> My spirit and my God shall be
> My seaward hill, my boundless sea."

Our working class, our poor, are yet more restricted in their vocations than the wealthy; they labour under far greater difficulties and disadvantages. The affluent are called upon to make some sacrifices, but the poor are often compelled to embrace means of livelihood that are altogether repugnant to their feelings and taste.

Fidelity to their religion and love of their kindred leaves them no alternative; and, alas! prejudice and ignorance have done their best to make their burden yet heavier and their fate sadder. Gifted men, and good men too, who have taken up the cause of suffering humanity, whose tender, brave, and earnest words have fallen like dew upon many a bruised heart, have yet made the toiling, suffering, but faithful Jew the butt of their wit and ridicule.

Authors, who from your pleasant homes looking out upon sunshine, who from your proud literary eminence send forth bitter words and envenomed shafts to wound and sting a very helpless fellow-creature, have you never understood that his wearisome life is not more to his taste than it would be to yours; that he does not love fog, and dirt, and darkness better than you would; but that a stern and sad necessity compels him to pursue a livelihood whose merit is that it gives food to the loved ones dependent on his exertions, and leaves him free to worship and obey the commandments of the God of his fathers. As he bends, together with his burden of old clothes, his steps to the light and airy suburbs that stretch around and beyond the homes of squalidness and darkness, do you not

think he longs to remove the pale wife and little
ones unto a clearer atmosphere, where summer's
fragrant breath would give them health and
vigour? He sees the rosy children standing at
their garden-gate, he sees the busy matron
breathing, as she works, the fresh sweet air, and
upon the old bag, the burden of years, falls a
tear, whilst, in the same monotonous voice, comes
the cry, "Old clo', old clo'." Novelists and
critics, the man whom you, in your pride or
your ignorance, deem so degraded and abject
(and yet upon whom you throw more and more
mire), that man may be performing life's task in
a nobler spirit than you whom the world reveres
as its teachers.

Thou takest a lowly place upon earth, toiling
Jew, poor clothesman, but in the day when the
heart's secret struggles and the mind's aspirations and its inner history shall be revealed, those
that are here the last, may be the first!

In passing different careers in review we find
that barriers still exist between the Jew and the
world, the eager-toiling, enthusiastic, fame-seek-
ing and fame-crowned world. These restric-
tions are differently received and met by different members of the Jewish community. Some,
but these are the smaller class, regard the sepa-

ration between them and their fellow-creatures with a feeling akin to exultation ; it is a badge of righteousness that they go abroad with ; a distinction that is a merit in their eyes. This class is composed of the rigid observers of outward forms and sanctities, whose piety is measured by the length of their prayers and by their scrupulous fidelity to the traditions of their rabbis. They are not disquieted by any aspirations after a more progressive life ; but are content to look backwards for instruction, and mould their present and their future by the past.

There is another class who retain of Judaism little or nothing but the name of Jew, who mingle freely with the world, and adopt any profession without religious scruple, and follow the business that holds out most advantages. They join occasionally in the solemnities of their faith, occasionally visit their synagogue, and this is enough to constitute them members of the community, and not unworthy ones either, if they are rich and liberal in their charities.

There is yet a third class comprising those that entertain a manly love for their religion, and who, whilst obeying its precepts, are not blind to the sacrifice it imposes. They recognise that they are living under the shadow of a dark dispensation, and feel, not without compunction, that the greatness that the world crowns with bay-leaves, that has statues erected to it, that receives the homage of an admiring senate, that is decorated with stars and rewarded by high-sounding titles, —that this greatness in its purple and glitter is not to be sought for nor to be obtained by the sincere and conscientious Jew.

But is no greatness possible? is there no path of fame open to the true disciple of Judaism? must the Jew remain stationary, whilst others progress around him? Is his natural ambition to be repressed, his manly hopes to be subdued? Shall he not take part in life's great battle and be a victor in the fight? Judaism answers this the mind's vehement cry, this its eager question; to her we must go for a solution of our difficulties. She tells us in solemn words that, whilst she imposes the sacrifice, she holds out a full compensation; that, whilst she closes many paths that stretch sparkling in sunshine before us, she invites us to others whose ascent may be steeper, but whose heights, once gained, place us on an eminence from whence we may see the storms of life waging beneath us.

She tells us that there is still sin and grief, a deep shadow over the world, and that this sin and sorrow arise from the false conceptions yet entertained of the Supreme Being and of man's duties to his Creator. She reveals God, the true God, to us, and the worship that He desires, and in this revelation are the elements of all true greatness, wisdom, and glory.

Religion has exercised and still exercises the deepest influence upon man; it is the great mover of human actions, and has played and still plays a great part in the history of the world. But religion, but faith, may be the demon as well as the angel of human life; it may lead to abysses of sin and misery, as well as to heaven and to God. When faith is the offspring of truth, she is a white-robed spirit, and bears the olive branch from the land of love across the troubled sea of life; but when she derives her being from fanaticism and superstition, then there is no deadlier or more malignant power; she spreads a funeral pall over the face of the earth, blots out God's daylight, silences thought, and forges chains, wherewith to hold free-born men and women in abject slavery.

In looking at the great map of history we see, here and there, luminous spots, that shine from out the surrounding darkness, and in these little spaces we find inscribed the names of men who

knew and served the true God.   The sages of
antiquity, whose memory is still revered, conceived in their age of superstition a truer idea of
the Almighty God than those around them; there
lay the secret of their superior wisdom : their country's deities were not deities to them ; their keener
vision pierced through the idolatry that shrouded
their land in darkness.   They saw enthroned in
light the one Infinite Being, they recognised the
Divine footprints upon the earth they trod, and
upon the sky they looked up to, and their minds
communed with the Eternal Mind.   In each successive age, under all churches, and amongst all
creeds, we find men whose noble minds, whose
sublime and heroic actions, stand out in beautiful
relief against the surrounding gloom ; men who
in the inner sanctuary of pure souls worshipped
the true God.

But these, unhappily, form the exception, for
few are the pages of the past and few the records
of the present that are not stained by tyrannical
decrees, by cruel actions, and by contemptible
lives, which owe their birth to a false faith and
a false worship ; thus we find recorded, as pro-
pitiatory offerings to the heathen gods, the sacrifice of human life at the shrine of Jupiter and
Vesta, the combats of the Coliseum, the death

struggles of maids and youths, of delicate matrons, of gray-haired men under the gripe of the beasts of the desert and beneath the eye of an applauding multitude. In later times, when Christianity was said to have civilized man, we see chronicled in characters of blood, and yet as religious acts, the massacre of St. Bartholomew, the expulsion from Spain of five hundred thousand men, women, and children, sent forth from their fatherland and homes, from prosperity and peace, to face exile, want, and death. In a further page we read, and still in the name of the Divinity, of the revocation of the edict of Nantes, which awoke from one end of France to the other a passionate despair; we see the tortures of the Inquisition; we see the lighted stakes, the blood-stained scaffolds, in the days of England's Mary; and thronged prisons within whose gloomy walls venerable priests, refusing to sacrifice their mind's integrity to the bigotry of James, sang their last hymn and breathed their last prayer on earth.

Drawing nearer to our own epoch, we find the Puritan's faith crushing happiness from out many a young heart, and paling the bloom of many a tender life. The voice of grief and despair mingled with the hymn of liberty, whose triumphal note awoke, upon the shores of New

England, the deep echoes which till that hour had slept in the bosom of eternity.

To the present day we still find that earth's saddest woes and darkest follies have their origin in a false conception of the Almighty God, and a false conception of the worship He demands from man. Hence the strife and bitter controversies between opposing sects—hence the bigotry and intolerance we find in all churches and in all creeds, that says to truth, like the Danish monarch said of old to the waves, " Thus far shalt thou go and no further." Alas! alas! what wrongs do we still see—what severing of nature's holiest ties—what happiness marred—what shadows cast even upon the domestic hearth—what resentments encouraged—what strife kindled—what enmity between brother and brother, friend and friend, and all perpetrated in the name of God! Horror upon horror! brought as offerings to the altar of the Eternal God. In reviewing the reign and decrees of religion (and what autocrat has ever swayed so great a power?) we arrive at this truth, that the highest knowledge and the greatest blessing man could possess would be the knowledge of the true God. Now Judaism reveals God to us, and therefore to her it is given to satisfy the deepest longing, the

purest aspiration, and the noblest of ambitions.
To her it is given to answer doubt, and scepti-
cism, and infidelity.   To her it is given to console the worn and weary, and lead mankind to
virtue, to honour, to an eternal glory.   Harmo-
niously as divinest music, majestically as the
thunder's boom, softly as the still small voice of
God, comes the blessed revelation across the lapse
of ages to us.

There is, says the voice, One Infinite and Eternal
Being, one God only, whose spirit fills all time and
all space, never embodied, but made manifest to
man in the glory of the Creation, in the majesty of
the starred spheres, in the sublime and unchang-
ing laws that govern the universe, in the solitude
of primeval forests, in the flower's delicate beauty,
in the green tree's early bloom, in the ocean's
grandeur, and in the joyousness of all living
things.

God is a spirit, says the voice, never embodied,
but realized to man through His moral attributes,
through love and mercy, through truth and holiness—a love and mercy whose depths know no
sounding, a truth which is the anchor of the universe, a holiness which radiates all things upon
which it shines.   God is a spirit, says the voice,
never embodied, but made known to man through

man's own affinity to God, through the mind, which is created in the image of the Divine mind. God is a spirit, says the voice, and is to be worshipped by the spiritual being with the soul and heart, with the intellect and affections. Love is to worshipped by love, mercy by mercy, holiness by holiness, and truth by truth. The inner being is to be consecrated to God, that is, consecrated to virtue, to humanity, to purity, moulded to the true image of the true God.

God is a spirit, says the voice, and He is the "Father of the spirits of all flesh," of the Jew and Christian, of the barbarian in his rude island home, of the Brahmin praying beneath his palm-tree, of the slave groaning under his heavy yoke. All human beings form part of His universal family, all are alike created in His image, all are sustained, loved, and redeemed by the eternal Lord and Father. He is Creator and King, Judge and Saviour. He is enthroned in heaven above, and dwells in every heart. He is the loving, merciful Father of the human race.

Do we hear this voice above the harsh warfare of contending creeds and opinions, above the invectives of fanaticism and intolerance ? Do we hear it above the world's revelry, above the roar of chariot wheels and gilded carriages ? Do we

hear it above the wail of anguish, above the cry
of the oppressed and enslaved ? Do we hear its
loving peace-breathing accents, or are they lost
amidst the tumult that fills the earth with a vain
clamour or a passionate grief ?

When the solemn revelation was proclaimed
to the wearied pilgrims that stood in trembling
awe around Mount Sinai, they did not feel its full
glory. The slaves of yesterday could not realize
the moral power and liberty, or the spiritual
greatness, that Judaism came to bestow upon
man. They did not see, as its hallowed words
fell upon the silent air, that the parched desert
and the rocky soil grew resplendent in beauty
and fertility. There was still a mist over their
eyes, and a shadow upon their hearts. Moses
stood alone at that hour, alone he felt its rapture and its blessing, alone he understood that
Judaism came not only to emancipate the bondsmen of Egypt from slavery, but the whole
human family from a yet sadder bondage, from
a false faith and false worship. Alone he understood that Judaism came to teach man that
virtue is the worship, that humanity is the prayer,
that obedience to the laws of nature, that self-
discipline and self-denial, that tolerance, for-

giveness, and mercy, are the sacrifices to be offered up to the true God.

Alone he understood that Judaism, which proclaimed man's spiritual affinity to the Divine mind, came to exalt and hallow the whole human race, and link all human beings together in the common love and common worship of the " Father of the spirits of all flesh."

Throughout the history of the Hebrews we still find that, even in the fatherland, whose every valley and hill spoke of God, of His love, His truth and mercy, few except the Psalmist and the prophets grasped the realities of Judaism ; and to the present day, whilst many fulfil its subordinate ordinances, its outward rites and ceremonies, instituted as sentinels to protect the inner treasure, few have conceived or realized, in their sublime length and breadth, its truth of truths, its divine spiritual law. We have, it is true, forsaken idolatry, as the word is commonly understood ; we dedicate our house of prayer to one God only, but is that God the true God ? The mind's temple may be filled with Deity or enshrine one image only, but the many and the one may alike be false. Do we feel that from God's unity emanates the power, the joy, and the redemption that sustains the whole universe, and blesses all mankind? Do we feel that the Eternal One is Creator, King, God, Father, and Saviour of all people? and, feeling this, are all men dear and holy to us? Do we feel that in God abides, and from Him proceeds, an infinite love and mercy, holiness and truth? and, feeling this, do we adore Him from and through these attributes? If not, we still worship a false God; and then in what are we better than idolators? Again, it is true that for many centuries we have obeyed the commandment of the Pentateuch, not to make or to bow down to any image of the Divinity, but have we understood by this that materialism is to be destroyed from out the sanctuary, as well as gold and clay and sculptured images of the invisible God? Have we not made our Judaism a creed composed of rites and ceremonies rather than a spiritual religion, an outward rather than an inner law?

Many of us fast and feast, and pray, and build and endow synagogues, present them with elaborately-adorned scrolls of the law, in which we write the first and last words. Many of us observe the Sabbath with a puritanical severity, carrying no weight, dipping no pen in ink, kindling no light. Many of us sweep all leaven from

our houses at Passover, and scrupulously observe
in all the festivals the minutiæ that tradition
has handed down to us; but few of us hold
communion with God in the wide temple of His
universe, or in the secrecy of our hearts; few
hear His voice in the voice of nature, or in the
dictates of their reason and their conscience;
few feel His presence above, around, and within
them; few perceive the glory that His presence
sheds upon all creation, the sanctity with which
it endows all human life, and the solemnity and
calm that it diffuses over the world, over its warfare, its sorrows, and its joys.

Few strive earnestly and evermore to mould
their inner being to the image of God, aspiring
day by day to a purer love, a deeper mercy, and
a wider truth.

Few recognise in every man, no matter how
poor, how fallen, or how begotten, born under
what clime or church, a child of God, and, as
such, respect his rights, his independence, and
his freedom. Few speak brave and earnest words,
and fewer still perform brave and earnest deeds.
Few sacrifice their worldly interest to their mind's
integrity or their soul's truth.   Materialism, the
great antagonist of Judaism, is still the crowned
chief of our community, and we must dethrone

the usurper before we can hope to realize a true faith or a true worship.

The lives of most of us are devoted to a vain ambition, to the acquisition of money, more and more money, or they are chilled by a profound religious apathy, or they are made contemptible by a puerile and skin-deep sanctity. We yet ignore the spiritual life, the life consecrated to God, to the mind's progress, to the soul's free communion with the beautiful, the true, the holy, and eternal. As in the history of the past the faith of Sinai is not yet understood, the sublime words of the Pentateuch, the sweet songs of the Psalmist, are echoed back from the walls of our synagogue, but they awake no deep echo in our hearts. Descendants of Egypt's bondsmen, of Judea's princes and priests, suffering and dispersed race, is not the mist still over your eyes and the shadow upon your hearts?

A true Judaism, a Judaism that the human soul in its loftiest inspiration, that nature in her beauty, that the Ancient Volume reveals to us, would make us, small community as we are, great and glorious. It would give us a stronger power than that wielded by despots on their thrones, or by armed forces, or by a vigorous nation's sturdy will. It would be the power of

truth over error, of a spiritual faith over the
world's materialism and infidelity; it would be
the power of mercy and tolerance over prejudice
and bigotry.   It would be a power whereby we
should lead men to the one true God, not through
violence and persecution, not through fear and
cowardice, not through the agency of priestcraft,
and miracles, and wonders working on feeble
and prostrate minds, but by a ministry of love
and truth, by the example of lives embodying the
Divine attributes.

As the disciples of a true Judaism a great
change would be effected amongst us; another
spirit would pervade our community, our institutions, our homes, our nurseries and schools, our
synagogues, our vocations, and our professions.
Religion would then perform her great part in
our lives.   She would not any more be dressed
up in false attire or false colours; she would not
be grim, or austere, or hypocritically bland; she
would not be brought forward on especial occa-
sions, on fast and feast days only, but she would
go, with her calm beauty and her majestic glory,
hand in hand with us through the world, from
the cradle to the grave.   Our children's education would be based upon religion, not the once
or twice a week Hebrew lesson, not the mas-

ter's preparation for the thirteenth birthday, not reciting the Hebrew blessings, not in the study of rabbinical lore only, but the religion of the heart and mind. It would be the mother's first teaching, the father's most solemn lesson. Our children would be taught by example and by precept that the highest wisdom and glory is the knowledge of the true God. They would be taught that to love Him and to deserve His love, to know His moral attributes and to emulate them, is life's most glorious and most solemn task. They would be taught that God is not to be mocked by an external or a skin-deep worship; that all ceremonies, all forms and rites, are to be looked upon only as means, not ends, of no value in themselves, save as they are moral helps, and as they awaken in us a stronger virtue, a deeper religious feeling. They would be taught to look to and investigate nature as a revealer of God's truths; they would be taught to look into their own hearts for God's inspirations and laws; they would be taught to read, to understand, and to interpret for themselves the Ancient Volume, so that theirs might be not a dead but a living faith; not another man's sanctity and obedience, but their own; not a second-hand religion, but one born out of their own hearts and

minds, implanted and rooted in their inner
being; finally, they would be taught that Judaism is to be exercised in the world, in the
field of labour, in their every-day life; that it is
to make them loving, merciful, true, and holy,
through their week's toil and their week's pleasures; that it is to make them remember, year by
year and day by day, their mind's affinity to God,
their brotherhood to the whole human race, and
their hope of immortality.

As disciples of a true Judaism we should no
longer pay to wealth the homage it has hitherto
received; not considering or seeking it for ourselves as the first and greatest object, we should
not make so many sacrifices for its acquisition.
The old idol thrown down, our social and our
mercantile life would assume a higher and
nobler aspect. We should not barter our independence or our integrity for any worldly advantage. We should remain true to ourselves,
even when our truth and integrity stood in
the way of self-aggrandizement. We should
make the life of business, the merchant's, the
trader's, the shopkeeper's, the general dealer's,
honourable and beautiful, through the lofty
morality, the uncorruptible principle, that would
pervade all our schemes and transactions.

" Sharp and clever as a Jew," or, " rich as a Jew," is now the common saying ; then it would be, " true and honest and upright as a Jew."

Again, when under the influence of a true Judaism, we should select far more often than now vocations in which we might embody the ideal and spiritual. When living more immediately in the presence of God, the true God, when holding communion with the Divine and Eternal, our minds would become more elevated and our aspirations nobler. To give expression to these aspirations would be a desire and a necessity of our lives. Then poets and painters, then sculptors and musicians would arise amongst us, whose ministry it would be to clothe in words, to breathe in melody, to portray on canvas, and to chisel from out marble, their own varied conceptions of the true and beautiful, of the pure and holy. They would be great teachers of great truths. When the heart and mind are inspired by a deep religious sentiment, when the love of the Divine and the enthusiasm of virtue kindle the flame of genius, then the poet becomes a priest. As an instance of this, the Psalms stand revered to the present day. How many human hearts have they not sustained and cheered, guided and strengthened ! How many, and how many weary, toiling, suffering, tempest-tossed human beings have they not saved from despair and shipwreck!

" David," says Ecclesiasticus, " David in all his works praised the Holy One Most High with words of glory, with his *whole heart he sang songs* and loved him that made him." And, because the royal Psalmist thus sung of God, and thus loved Him with all his heart, have those thrilling, solemn, tender hymns outlived three thousand years, and will still continue to exist as long as the human soul knows hope and fear, grief and joy, and seeks as its refuge and its friend the Divine and Eternal.

The harp of Zion has long been mute, but its chords might sound again melodious as of old, though, perhaps, with a more mournful cadence than in the fatherland, if, as the sweet singer of Israel, we but loved and served the Almighty Father with all our heart, if our whole being felt and did homage to His glorious moral attributes.

The same may be said of the artist as of the poet: his works, when inspired by a true religious feeling, will make him a teacher of mankind. The artist draws back the veil that covers truth; he portrays nature and humanity as they are seen by the spiritual eye; he does not invent or enrobe imaginary figures or scenes or give us the fictitious colours of fancy, but presents reality to us—a reality that is not discovered by the common worldly eye, for this perceives but the superficialities, the shams, and shows of life, whilst the spiritual eye penetrates beneath the surface, and sees the true and lasting, the noble and eternal. Very dark and unsightly is the oyster-shell, very beautiful the pearl; so is it with humanity, often rude and rough in its exterior, but beautiful in its inner depths. This the artist, inspired by a pure Judaism, would reveal to us, for he would feel it himself deeply and truly, and he would stamp it upon his canvas, now in one form, now in another, but still teaching the same truth.

It is a lesson that we stand much in need of, for, owing, perhaps, to the evil influence of centuries of persecution and degradation, the Jews have lost much of their faith in the beauty and nobleness of human nature; they have lost the deep respect and reverence that man, as the noblest work of God's creation, is entitled to, an unconditional respect and sympathy as regards external circumstances, founded on each human mind being created in the image of God. They look to the outer man, to his position, to his

gold and his silver, and respect him more or less
as these are more or less considerable.   There is
a sad deficiency of poetic thought and feeling
amongst us, and their want is felt whenever we
leave our mercantile life.   As long as we are in
the city, trading, buying, and selling, we have
great power, but there our power ceases; our
imagination and feelings have yet to be aroused
and enlisted in the cause of religion ; the service
of the head without the heart is very inadequate.
Whenever the Jewish heart awakens to a true
love of the true God, then we shall produce great
works, works that shall be benefactors of mankind,
and that shall endure through time to eternity.

Again, as true disciples of the faith of Sinai,
we should esteem as the most honourable of all
vocations one that is now held but in poor repute
amongst us.

At present no English gentleman of any standing educates his child for the pastor's office.
Either foreigners are selected to be our rabbis,
or they are chosen from amongst our poorer
class, and receive at the hands of charity but an
inferior education.

Were Judaism a living faith amongst us, and
her precepts a living law, it would be deemed a
glorious mission to preach the truths eternal, to

lead men to the knowledge of the Almighty God
and Father. It would be deemed a happy mission to consecrate one's life to the ministry of
religion; to impart fresh zeal and energy to the
weary and worn; to awaken a solemn repentance
and a solemn hope in the forsaken, the degraded,
and guilty; to throw down the idols of the rich
and the sensual, and help them to enthrone the
true Divinity in their souls. It would be deemed
a noble mission to stand by the suffering and
dying, and when human nature is weakest give
it the support of religion, of God's love and God's
mercy; and, when the darkness of death is gathering round, to bring the light of God's love and
God's mercy to shine upon the parting soul and
reveal Heaven to it. Men of high social position
men of intellectual and moral greatness, would
embrace the pastor's life, and make it noble and
great through a pure and sublime faith.

Then, also, we should have a larger body of
philanthropists among us : men and women, who,
looking upon every child of earth as the noblest
work of God's creation, as claiming a spiritual
affinity to the Eternal Mind, as forming part of
the great brotherhood, would devote their moral
and intellectual powers to the welfare and progress of their fellow-creatures. In this vocation

there need be no barrier between Jew and Christian, they could work heart to heart and hand in hand. There are great wrongs to redress, there are great evils to eradicate, in which task they both might join beneath a broad banner of love and mercy.

In our own community there is still much to be done. We feed the starving, we shelter the houseless, we spend large sums on charitable institutions, but few devote their best energies towards securing a permanent good for their poorer brethren. We rather seek to alleviate than effectually to cure distress; we are more solicitous to provide them with a temporary relief than to raise their social position and place them altogether above the reach of want. We compassionate our poor for living and dying in homes of darkness, for bequeathing, by so doing, impaired constitutions and weakened minds to their children, but the compassion has hitherto borne no fruit. When the brotherhood of a true Judaism, that brotherhood that asks for a love akin to that we bear ourselves, is understood and practised, we shall do more than idly deplore an evil affecting so many; we shall remedy it, or at least strive to do so, with heart and soul. The poor of themselves have no alternative but to renounce their religious duties, or remain from youth to age in the close dark alleys of the city : but the wealthy might remedy this ; there are several plans that might be realized by which the poor might, at least, occasionally enjoy, what to the rich appears a *necessity*, the blessings of country air, of summer's sunshine and gladness. An industrial school might be erected in some salubrious and picturesque site near London, where our young would thrive physically and morally better than in the close purlieus of the metropolis. A synagogue might be attached to it, and the children's religious education be carefully attended to. The teachers, cheered and elevated by scenes of beauty and repose, and by receiving themselves daily lessons from the works of God, would acquire a higher knowledge and holier feelings than they have hitherto possessed. Their teaching would be fraught with a new power, and they would send forth into our community a hardier and a nobler race—men and women who would infuse a fresher and a healthier spirit amongst our poor. A few visits to our poor brethren would prove to any one how much physical vigour, and strength, and moral power is needed amongst our working classes. Such pale care-worn faces, such thin, weakly, and stunted forms are found in their dark homes; and prejudices and superstition throw an additional gloom over dwellings already gloomy enough.

The future generation might be very different if the children of to-day were brought up under happier influences. Again, some convalescent infirmary might be established in the country, where the weak and weary might renovate their health and strength.

What happiness, after a painful confinement to a close dark home, and to a long solitude within sound of the city's perpetual noise and bustle, to breathe the fresh air, to hear the sweet music, the soft loving voice of nature! What happiness to look up into the deep blue sky stretching far into a sea of boundless light around them, to sit beneath the shade of verdant trees, to inhale the perfume of flowers, to feel the coolness of dewy fields upon their parched lips and fevered brow! Then, as health returned, what happiness to wander at will into meadow paths, to saunter along scented hedges, to penetrate into tangled copse, or follow the silver thread of tiny rivulet, now through green vale and mossy dell, and now upward to the wood-crowned hill where its waters derive their source; what a delight to quaff a full draught of that untainted

stream from its pellucid spring! Would not such
seasons be remembered by our poor as a new
starting-point in life from which God was to be
better loved and better served? The Psalmist's
thrilling anthems of praise and adoration, inspired by nature's loveliness and glory, by the
Eternal Father's works, must be a dead letter
now to most of our poor. The purest of all
religious emotions, that which is awakened by
the sight of the beautiful, the calm, and sublime
in nature, is unknown to them. Can we be surprised if their religion is more ceremonial than
spiritual, if they pray more with the lips than
with the heart? How little is done to make them
know God, the true God, the great and beneficent
Creator, the loving and merciful Father! Walls,
walls of brick and stone, ever between them and
nature ; walls, walls of brick and stone, between
them and sunshine, and too often walls of pride
and arrogance between them and the hearts of
earth's happier children.

Again, some broad lands might be purchased
and a Jewish colony established on the soil ; the
house of prayer, the children's school, the aged
parents whose presence hallows the hearth of
the young, might be gathered there, and the
Jewish agriculturist might plough and sow his

land and reap his harvest in cheerfulness and peace, in truth and virtue. Are these idle visions, or will they not, must they not, become realities, whenever we realize a true and living Judaism; whenever its precepts become the law of our moral being, whenever it is understood that our love of God must be tested by our love of our fellow-creatures and that we serve and worship Him whenever we serve His children? Other evils under which our community now suffer might be mentioned; but the remedy for one is the remedy for all—a true religion and a true faith, which would inspire us with the sympathies, the energy, and will, whereby we should work out the real good and ensure the real welfare of our brethren.

Other pursuits and professions open to the Jew might be enumerated; but enough has been said to show that lives of usefulness and beauty, lives dear to the good and dear to God, may be embraced by the faithful disciples of a true Judaism. Amidst these vocations we should have little time or inclination to regret those denied to us, or rather, in the heart's deep peace, in the mind's harmony, in the soul's calm hope, the result of our true faith, the world's distinctions and honours would be forgotten. We should be

looking up to a greater Master; we should be
looking forward to a higher glory.   Men hitherto have gloried in many things, in their wisdom,
in their learning, in their wealth, and in their
power; our glory would be our knowledge and
our worship of the true God—the God not of
Jew or Christian only, but the God of the universe, the Father of the spirits of all flesh, the
God of an infinite truth and love and holiness
and mercy, and whose worship is faith and holiness, mercy and love.   In this knowlege and this
worship we might feel, and rejoice to feel, that we
could not be left behind in the march of human
progress; but that we should pioneer the way to
paths of truth and happiness.   By our pure conception of the divinity and spiritual worship of
the Eternal Father, by a loving and merciful faith,
by an enlightened and living Judaism, we should
impart sublime truths, and by our example, by
our precepts, and by our works, cast an unfading
lustre upon this enterprising and eager, upon this
great and noble age.

CHAPTER II.

GOD'S TRUTH AND MAN'S TRUTH.

" For ever, O Lord, thy word is established in heaven; thy
faithfulness is unto all generations." " Thy word is true
from the beginning, and thy righteous judgment endureth
for ever." " The works of God's hands are verity; his commandments are sure. They stand fast for ever and ever,
and are done in truth and uprightness."—*Psalms.*

THE whole universe is illumined by God's truth-
revolving spheres, the skies, the earth, human
life, and human destiny are made bright and
beautiful by the Creator's eternal faithfulness.
We look up to nature as to a friend, because
her great Master has made her works, works of
truth. We feel that her sunshine and her loveliness, that her power and sublimity are all true,
that she charms by no false smiles, allures by no
false colours, puts forth no assumption that she
cannot carry out, and no power that she cannot
vindicate—and so we love and confide in nature,
repose upon her breast as upon a mother's, and

listen to her lessons as to a safe and holy
teacher.

Our religious faith reposes upon God's immutable truth ; the immortal and spiritual being
derives his moral glory from his inmost conviction of the truth of the Divinity, the Divinity
that is above, around, and within him. It is the
anchor of the hopes that are shared by all mankind, the deep, unfathomable hopes we all entertain of the existence of a Supreme Being, of an
over-ruling Providence, and of the immortality
of man.

Judaism is built upon the verity of God's
Word. Since the Law was proclaimed amidst the
thunders of Sinai, and the loving covenant sealed
between the Almighty Father and the released
bondsmen of Egypt, centuries have passed away.
Since the light of that moral revelation dawned
upon the wilderness, what changes and revolu-
tions has time not effected ! Since then nations
have risen into greatness and sunk into oblivion ;
empires have been established and have declined ;
creeds after creeds have erected altars on which
they have shrined their deities, and creeds, and
altars, and deities have been alike overthrown ;
whole races have been exterminated from off the
face of the earth ; whilst yet, amidst the havocs

and the wrecks of time, Judaism exists, for it is
founded upon an imperishable basis, God's infinite truth.   We, who are still the byword, the
proverb, the scorn and astonishment of the nations among whom our scattered race abide, and
who in many lands have yet to bear a heavy
burden of contumely and degradation, we may
well feel that we have no safe shelter but beneath
the wide-spreading wings of Eternal Faithfulness.
We know that, in spite of the tribulations that
sadden our career, in spite of the dense clouds
that shroud our horizon, that the glorious destiny predicted for Israel will yet be realized.
God's Word hath declared it, and in that Word
we may fully confide.

There are epochs in each man's life when the
deep waves of anguish overwhelm us, and at
such moments, tempest-tossed upon a wild sea
of grief, we might be led to question God's love
and mercy, but that His truth, immutable and
firm, rises above the depths of our despair, and
we cling to it, even as the shipwrecked mariner
clings to the plank that bears him through surg-
ing tides and battling waves in safety to the
shore.   Who has not felt, when trouble after
trouble has come upon us, when harassing cares
and anxieties have rapidly succeeded each other,

perplexing and haunting us with the dread of
yet greater and impending evils, who has not
felt that earth's burdens would be too great to
bear had we not God as a stronghold and a
refuge? did we not know that all His promises to
those who suffer in meekness and in patience
will be fulfilled? did we not feel assured that
those who sow in tears shall reap in joy? and in
this full conviction of God's truth the weary
mind and heart are soothed and strengthened.
Who also, whilst watching the ebbing life of the
long-loved and loving, have not felt their own
life grow cold within them, and the pulses of
their hearts stayed by the freezing grasp of a
withering despair; and then at the thrilling remembrance that the departing are not lost, but
returning to the God of truth, who also has not
felt their whole being awake again to life, to
hope, even to a solemn joy, a hallowed rejoicing
that the dear one will be safe and free at last?
Thus we may say with the Psalmist, in the
agony of our bereavement and in the conflict
of our trials, " Thy mercy, O God, is above
the heavens; thy truth reacheth unto the
clouds."

In contemplating and adoring the Eternal
Faithfulness, upon which we build, as on a rock,

our hopes both in time and in eternity, we are
led to ask ourselves, Is man's truth in harmony
with nature's truth and with God's truth? Do
we render back to the Almighty some portion of
the truth with which He blesses us? Do we
give our fellow-creatures some measure of that
truth that God bestows upon His children? This
divine attribute of the Supreme Being has been
clearly and fully revealed to us, has been con-
spicuously displayed in all God's works, that it
may become the great example of our lives, the
authority whose guiding influence we acknowledge and whose dictates we obey. As crystal
waters reflect the orb of day, so should the
human mind, transparent as pellucid stream,
reflect God's truth; and as the sun dispels surrounding fog and mist, so should God's truth,
the light of His moral universe, dissipate the
mental and the moral clouds that would otherwise shroud us in darkness. Without truth there
can be no spiritual affinity between man and his
Creator; it is the link that binds most indissolubly together the child of earth to the Almighty
Father; and this affinity is religion, is worship,
is prayer, is holiness and virtue. Truth is the
groundwork of all piety, the pedestal upon which
all virtue has to be raised. It is building upon

sand when we build upon any other foundation, it is placing ourselves at the mercy of every adverse wind, of every conflict and change. Without truth our minds become barometers, recording not our own principles and state, but the variations in the moral atmosphere around us, a continual shifting up and down, with little reference to the inner being's real thoughts or opinions.

As this is a world of probation and of discipline, in which we have to contend in order to conquer, in which we are assailed by temptations in order to gain strength and nobleness by resistance, so our rectitude is exposed to trial that it may be not the truth only of innocence and inexperience, but of dignity and principle, which knows what it embraces and what it relinquishes. We shall find it an arduous, though the noblest of tasks, to preserve, throughout our career, an unsullied integrity. The mind that, through an active and ambitious manhood, and through the weakness and weariness of age, has maintained a pure rectitude and a lofty independence, that mind has drawn near to the Divine Creator, has won for itself the most godlike quality—the quality that God displays to us as His most glorious attribute.

When, in the presence of Nature or beneath the influence of God's Word, we survey the majesty and beauty of truth, we can hardly understand how it is not the vital principle of our existence, the great law of our lives; but when, from the house of prayer, from the retirement of our thoughts, from the solitude or calm of green fields and meadows that smile up into God's heavens, we go back into the world to mingle in its warfare and its vanities, that which a little moment before we owned as supreme is forgotten, and our soul, so happy erstwhile in its freedom, submits itself once more to a tyrannical master. Unable to attain our worldly views or purposes without a deviation from truth, we assume a character and we play a part, or we put in the background and cover up the principles and the feelings that might, if discovered, mar our success.

The ambition of some individuals is to be looked up to as saints, is to play a conspicuous part in the religious world, and so the outward garb of sanctity is assumed, the public forms and rites of their creed are strictly performed, whilst the mind and heart are left in ignorance of its spirit, and the world perhaps applauds, whilst God is mocked by a hypocritical worship.

Wealth, with its pomp and luxuries, is the good coveted by others, and, in their endeavour to equal or outstrip in the race the competitors by whom they are surrounded, they have recourse to intrigue and to dissimulation. The warehouse, the wharf, the lawyer's office, the shop, the merchant's counting-house, how often are they the witnesses of crooked transactions and ignoble deceptions?

Others are eager to gain fame and distinction, and no matter how, so that the purpose is achieved, and the wreath, the trumpet praise, obtained; and in this struggle after earth's lofty honours, the bar, the senate, the pulpit even, send forth plausible, talented, and flattering but false arguments, pleadings, and doctrines, by which the golden meed is won, but the mind's rectitude is tarnished and its independence lost.

Others have no dearer object than to sail smoothly down the stream of life, to run upon no rocks, or to meet no counter current, so they choose a well-known course, where they can navigate their bark in ease, and glide along "With pleasure at the helm and youth at the prow;" whilst yet, perhaps, conscience not all asleep, a sense of duty not quite dormant, is urging them to another path. How many convictions true

and noble are thrust back into silence and darkness, because they are not expedient or safe, or
worldly wise or worldly useful! And the life
that might have been made honourable and great,
through maintaining and exposing these very convictions, becomes but a well-acted falsehood. Oh
world!—not God's earth, but man's world,—what
cowards and what renegades you make of us;
beneath your influence and your ministry what
a masquerade do we make of human life, going
to the very grave with a false reputation and a
false character, dressed up to the very last in a
contemptible disguise!

We, who are the disciples of a religion that
places us in the immediate presence of an all-see-
ing God, beneath the unslumbering eye of infinite
truth, we should, of all people, be the most faithful and zealous adherents of truth; yet unhappily,
most unhappily, circumstances over which we had
no control, have impaired that deep fidelity, that
perfect rectitude, which should have been Israel's
noblest inheritance—a bequest passing unsullied
and undiminished from father to son.

The persecution of centuries, the compulsion
and violence, the fierce bigotry and enmity, by
which we were assailed, have unfortunately too
often entailed upon us a love of mystery, a dex-

terity in trickery, and a pleasure in intrigue. We were hunted down, tracked like wild beasts from home to home, despoiled of our possessions, deprived of our prerogatives; our best, or indeed our only chance of safety was to wear a mask, was to conceal our religion, our name, and our fortune beneath an impenetrable mystery. We were compelled to worship God in the strictest seclusion, to offer up our united prayers in chambers where no windows opening to God's blue skies might betray our secret purpose, and to whisper, instead of singing with gladful voices, the choral anthems of praise and love, so that no sound of Hebrew psalm and melody might reach the outer air. We wore, so as not to attract attention, poor and faded garments in public, lived in mean-looking houses, and only when in the privacy of home could we assume the appearance and indulge in the luxury befitting our station. We adopted the ignoble callings that were thrown open to us, whilst we carried on beneath some disguise the vocation more suited to our tastes or talents, but which was interdicted by intolerance and by oppressive laws. We led, therefore, almost simul-taneously, two lives, one false, one real; but they necessarily mingled, the impure sullying the pure, the fictitious degrading the true. What at first was most painful or irksome, and felt and resented as a barbarous indignity, became less and less odious, as it developed by exercise fatal propensities and talents. A vice that grows, even though by necessity, familiar to us, soon ceases to be regarded as a vice; we learn to look upon it in another light and give it some other name. An evil, therefore, born and taken root amongst a people, who shall say to what extent it shall not spread, or when it will be exterminated?

In those dark and wretched ages money occasionally obtained for us the prerogatives which should only have been accorded to virtue, and money, naturally, became a first object; an idol that we enshrined in our hearts, and to which we paid an unworthy homage. The urgent necessity for wealth wherewith to satisfy the rapacity of kings and governments and the cupidity of a sordid priesthood, wherewith to purchase a temporary shelter and protection, has long since passed away. But the disposition, the taste, the love, that necessity awoke, and kept whetted so keenly, has not passed away: feelings are hereditary, and our affection and our reverence linger round the idol which still remains on its pedestal. The love of money, the fear and dread of poverty, that exist among us, are the chief causes that

lead us in the present day to deception and
falsehood.   They take away our independence,
and without independence there can be no truth.
The man whose dearest interests are his worldly
interests, whose highest aim in life is to increase
his store of worldly good, dare not act boldly,
dare not speak out bravely, dare not give expression to his inmost thoughts, or utterance to his
deepest convictions.   Truth might stand in the
way of his success, might prove obnoxious in
some influential quarter, might offend the patron
on whose interest his advance depends, and so it
is repressed and concealed, resigning its place to
subservience or flattery, or to a discreet reserve
which ever answers best the purpose of his personal aggrandisement.   We must learn to value
less earth's vanities and earth's grandeurs.   We
must learn to honour our fellow-creatures for
what they are, not for what they have.   We must
learn to see through their fine clothes or their
coarse garments, and put neither their poverty
nor their wealth, but their inner worth in the
scale when we weigh their merits.   Till we do
this we shall never put forth truth ourselves, or
see it realized in others.

The rich do wrong, very wrong, to blazon forth
their wealth, as if it brought them all the hap-

piness that its prospect holds out. They act a
falsehood by so doing, and a most pernicious one
to a large class of their brethren. They know,
by experience, that the power of money is, after
all, but a limited one, and that there are blessings
inumerable which wealth cannot purchase. They
know that bitter tears are shed in gorgeous
mansions; that the dullest moments are spent on
velvet sofas, and wearied hours by the side of
sculptured hearths, and that heavy aching hearts
are borne along in the gilded carriages that roll
so pompously past us. There is little, much too
little, intercourse between the different classes of
society, but that little would be of some avail
were it carried on in truth; but as it is, the rich
man spreads an untruth when he goes amongst
or calls his poorer brethren to him. He affects
an air of such superiority and grandeur that the
poor man can but believe that wealth exalts us
above the common evils of humanity, and he
must, as a necessary consequence, yearn to pro-
cure the good that thus appears to confer such
privileges, and bestow such immunities. Could
the poor man but see into the disquietudes of the
monied man's life, he might learn to be content
with a simple existence, and seek the true and
lasting, instead of running after shadows and

grasping at bubbles. Could we all, the affluent and the poor, but learn to estimate money at its real value, we should not any of us be in such a terrible hurry to get rich; and it is this eager haste, this trembling anxiety to secure the prize, that induces us to be little scrupulous about the ways and means we employ. We must climb the ladder of fortune as fast or faster than our neighbours, and in the steep ascent who shall say what false steps are not taken, what slips are not made? but when the summit is gained few among us care to know or to remember what sacrifices of honesty and independence have been made, what dereliction of principle it has cost, and what stain it has left upon our integrity.

But it is time to rouse ourselves from this artificial state, to wake up from these illusions, shake off these fictions; for, however much our deeds may contradict it, and our course deny it, life is indeed real, and God is indeed truth. We may for a time be successful actors; we may assume a religious badge to which we have no real claim; we may earn a reputation that is not deserved; we may wear the wreath that should bind another's brow; we may openly sanction that which our hearts condemn; we may take unfair advantages of our weaker brethren; we may make

capital profits and laugh at the purchaser : we
may do all this, and yet life is real, for the hour
must come when all this acting must cease, when
our fictitious parts are played, and we see that
they have been played in vain. Time, sickness,
grief, and death will find us out, in spite of all
disguise ; they are life's great realities, from which
we cannot hide ourselves, and which strip us bare
of all self-illusions and all deceptions. Time dis-
covers us beneath wigs, and flowing locks, and
painted cheeks, beneath the affected airs and
graces of youth. There is no staying the dial
that marks our onward course to age and the
grave ; grief is arrested by no walls, no retinue of
domestics ; it opens the latch of the cottage door
and enters in at the palace portal, where the
armed sentinel vainly keeps guard. Silently,
but solemnly, it holds up to our view the mirror
of truth, through which, perhaps, we had not
gazed for years. The happy and prosperous may
keep it out of sight ; but sorrow and adversity
rend the veil, and once more we stand face to
face with truth. Should Time even deal gently
with us and grief be spared, still Death, mysterious Death, must come, sooner or later, to perform, and that less gently and less gradually,
their task and ministry. When we stand upon

the threshold of Eternity, we shall feel, that though we enacted a false part on earth's passing scenes, yet life was real. At that supreme hour all our counterfeit virtues will stand before us as forgeries, and the false words, the false deeds, that have dishonoured our lives with their meretricious colours and their hollow sounds, will rise up, phantom like, to haunt and accuse us. We shall then feel, what perhaps we knew, but never felt before, that nothing false may stand in the presence of God ; that we must all appear without disguise or semblance, what and as we really are, before the tribunal seat of judgment. What, then, to us man's golden opinions—what, then, the full coffers—what, then, the costly luxuries— what, then, the subservience of the multitude— what, then, the patron's favour—what, then, the rich man's smile or the world's adulation—what, then, any of the possessions for which we bartered our rectitude, compromised our honesty, and sold our independence? A true heart, a true mind, a true holiness, a true charity, a true life, erring and frail perhaps, yet true, would then outweigh in our estimation all earth's treasures ; for these, and these alone, may be offered by man to the Almighty Father, or will be accepted by the God of Eternal Truth. Before it is too late, before the final summons comes, let us feel that life is real; that we were not intended to be actors but real and earnest beings, performing a real and earnest part, beings who feel the sublimity of truth, the utter vanity and degradation of all deception.

It is indeed time for us to break through the bondage that has placed us under the yoke of falsehood, for, gild it as we may, we are in many respects still slaves, more to be pitied than the bondsmen of Egypt, for they wore the galling chain around their bodies, whilst we drag its iron weight around our minds. Here in this dear land of liberty, our free England, no violence, or compulsion, or interdict enslaves us more. Here—where all men are free to follow the dictates of their conscience—here our worship may represent our belief, our words may be the echo of our thoughts, and our actions the outward manifestation of our inner principles. Virtually and morally free, we need never more desecrate our minds and hearts by guile or by falsehood; we need never more be guilty of such a despicable meanness towards our fellow man, of such a cowardly weakness to ourselves and such a blasphemy to God, as acting a false part and living a false life. This happy change in our

social position not only allows us to throw off
the mask we once were compelled to wear, but it
opens a wide sphere of duty to us, calls upon us
to search for truth, to explore her paths, and
sound her depths.   She has a harvest prepared
for us all, but we must all go forth as gleaners
in her fields, or labourers in her mines, and
gather her treasures for ourselves.

If we care at all for our intellectual and spiritual progress, this must be our first task; we
must no longer be content with the opinions and
decisions of others, but investigate ourselves what
interests us most closely and dearly.   This work
of examination regards most especially our religious faith; it can only be real and noble when
it is the deliberate conviction and the innate sentiment of our mind.   Another man's creed forced
upon us or blindly adopted can be of no avail.
It is not enough to be a Jew, because our father
was a Jew before us, but Judaism, to be anything,
must be a truth to the individual, a living, glorious truth, to whose fulfilment he can consci-
entiously devote his life.   We each must read the
Bible for ourselves, and for ourselves recognise
its revelation and accept its precepts.   Our brother's faith, however great and true, cannot carry
any one but himself to heaven.   It is not the

faith, either, that singly will be judged of by
God, or proclaimed either right or wrong, but
the earnestness and sincerity of the believer,
the truth with which he has embraced and
the purity with which he has practised his
religion. When our faith has been earnestly
sought for and received, then it inspires us with
a holy zeal that achieves wonders for ourselves
and for mankind; but when we only adopt the
popular faith because it is the faith of the multitude, or that in which we were born, then it
works no miracles for ourselves or our brethren;
then it leaves us as it found us, apathetic and
indifferent, or scoffers and infidels at heart. No
scientific lore, no profound and abstruse learning,
no college education, are required in the fulfilment of this, man's most sacred task; nothing is
wanted but the love of God, which is the love of
truth. Simple labourers, toiling mechanics, poor
artisans, toiling wives and mothers may engage
in the work, along with the erudite scholar,
the proficient, the skilled or monied man, the
woman of fashion and the gifted matron. Let
it not be said that there is too much ignorance
amongst our working class for them to search
for and find truth for themselves. It would be
a lamentable confession, a most deplorable evil,

crying loudly for redress, if correct. But happily, it is not the case; we have but to acquire for ourselves, to give, and to honour independence in others, and there will be no deficiency of mental power and accurate judgment amongst any of us. God has endowed all men with the faculty of reflection, and with a free will; He therefore has given them, at the same time, the capability to think and investigate, and the power to carry out their opinions and manifest them to the world.

A lofty spirit, a brave heart, and a staunch mind,—these are requisite in our search after truth, for she inhabits perilous haunts, now dwelling in deep caverns, now upon mountain heights, now in close citadels, now in lone primeval solitudes, and now in the tumultuous world. Sometimes huge dark figures stand menacingly before these homes, and with fierce mien and gestures wave us back. Grim superstition, intolerance, and bigotry are the enemies of truth, and seek to arrest our onward progress. They attack us with the subtle arms of sophistry and doubt, and kindle fierce flames around our path. Sometimes, instead of gaunt opponents offering us battle, our steps are waylaid by sirens, who with music and song seek to beguile us from our lofty enterprise. Pleasure, fame, and wealth, crowned with flowers and glittering in sunshine, tempt us from our purpose, and, beneath the influence of their smiles, truth is too often forgotten or betrayed.

We have, therefore, to combat, to struggle, to resist, and to watch. We have to acquire a spirit of self-denial and self-abnegation; we have to nerve ourselves so that we may tread rough paths and cross dreary tracts, so that we may wear the martyr's robe and sustain the martyr's conflict. In this search after truth, and in this adoption of truth, we shall have to bear at times the contempt and the disapprobation of the world, at times its ridicule and laughter. We shall have at times to renounce wealth or distinction, we shall have to oppose and uproot, and we shall have to plant and build up.

We may have to relinquish what once we loved and revered; we may have to give up the shelter of old and time-honoured sanctuaries, to take shelter only in our own integrity and in God's truth. For, in being true to ourselves, to our fellow man, and to the Almighty God, we shall be exposed to many trials and many griefs. We may be sorely tempted at times to put on a disguise again to pursue the winding easy path instead of the straight and rough one; to follow the multitude, instead of treading a lonely path ; to purchase cheaply the world's benefits, instead of striving to win an immortal but a hidden treasure. Yet let us not fail : we have borne much and made many sacrifices, toiled and laboured in the attainment of transient good and failing honour ; shall we hesitate, when the object is an imperishable one, when it confers upon us man's loftiest prerogative, an assimilation and an affinity to the Eternal Father ?

For the sake of all that is great and good, for the sake of the divine in our human nature, for the sake of Judaism, the pure and noble revelation sullied and brought low through our sin and degradation, for the sake of the Almighty Father whose love is round us still, and who would redeem His children, let us become the disciples of truth, of God's own glorious and infinite truth. Let us uphold her cause, speak her brave words, and perform her enduring deeds. Let us earnestly and solemnly resolve to devote our intellectual and moral powers to the acquisition of truth ; let us deem no labour, no effort, and no sacrifice too considerable.

In selecting a profession let us see if its practice is compatible with our truth, and should it, upon a careful examination, not prove so, let it be relinquished, however lucrative, or worldly honourable, or worldly noble it seems. Before entering into any engagement, political or commercial, let us see if it might impair our rectitude or weaken our mind's independence; and if there is any chance of such a result, let it be renounced, however brilliant, or plausible, or advantageous its acceptance appears. Before pledging ourselves in any wise, let us see that the pledge may be given with a perfect integrity. Let no words of a false friendship pass between man and man, no oily phrases, no sycophant flattery, no hypocritical deference, beneath which, as under a safe shelter, enmity, envy, and distrust may lurk. Let not the marriage altar be profaned by the false vows of a false love. Let not the young girl, for all the wealth and grandeur, and all the pomp of earth, barter her truth and freedom. Never let her young mind and heart be polluted by the putting on the semblance of an affection and devotion that do not exist. Let her remember that if in this, the most important act of her life, she is untrue, in all probability her career will be one of deception and guile. Untrue in this, her holiest relation in life, she will be untrue in others, and no after tears and after regret shall ever altogether wash away the dark stain left upon her soul's integrity.

Let the education we give our children be based upon real principles and real feeling. Let our little ones be cradled in truth, and reared in an atmosphere of truth, so that it may become their natural element in which they alone can breathe freely. Let there be no deceit between mother and child. There should be nothing through which a child can see so transparently as its mother's heart and mind. Let it see that the smile that lights up her face is the reflection of the sunshine of her heart, and that the soft gentle voice is the outward expression of kind and harmonious feelings. Let it see that the benevolence talked of abroad is followed up at home by acts of patient forbearance and self-denial. Let it see that, amidst the warfare of conflicting opinions and arguments, it is indeed truth that is sought and battled for; not dominion, or intolerance, or party spirit that is waging war under a false name and a false pretence. We would say to all parents, in contradiction to Shakspeare's Hamlet, "Assume no virtue if you have it not;" but strive, but struggle, but pray for the attainment of those qualities you wish your

children to emulate.   You will but be nobler in
their eyes for the effort they see you make to
obtain the mastery over faults and passions that
the clear-sighted eye of youth will discern, even
though you attempt to deny their existence, or
put forth virtues to which you have no real
claim.   Your earnest striving after a higher moral
perfection, your open acknowledgment of errors,
your contrition for short-comings, will inspire
them with a deeper, purer love of the good, the
noble, and the holy, than all your shams and
illusions, and all your assumptions of virtues that
you do not in reality possess.   Above all, let
your children see that all your religious practices
are the result of an earnest faith, that your private and your public worship are one and the
same thing, springing from the same source, directed to the same end, the true love and true
service of the Almighty Father.

Let us, one and all—rich and poor, men of all
professions, women of all grades, fathers and
mothers, youth and age—remember that the God
who never slumbers—that the God who reads the
human heart in all its mysteries, and in all its
workings—from whose presence, nor disguise, nor
night, nor darkness shall hide us—that the God
before whose throne we must all appear and

render up an account of the life given us—that this God is a God of truth. That the light of His creation, that the splendour of His firmament, that the music of His spheres, that the ministry of His angels, that the rapture and the beatitude of heaven is truth, and that nothing but truth shall abide in the glory of His presence. Let us remember this through our joyous and untrammelled childhood, through our eager and restless manhood, and through our stricken and feeble age. Let us remember it through all our pursuits and vocations, through all our joys and sorrows, through all our difficulties and temptations. Let it be the solemn thought of our lives, at once our guardian and our monitor. Let it be so present to our minds that we may make it our most earnest endeavour, our earliest and latest task, to be true men and true women, men and women who, through all the warfare and all the revelry of the world, hear the voice of conscience, " the still small voice of God," and who, through glitter and pomp, or through penury and abject-ness, see the beauty and the divinity of truth.

A few even of such faithful adherents and such noble champions of truth would work out great and salutary reforms. A few true hearts and minds amongst us would effect what no

number without truth could do. A few true
hearts and minds would suffice to restore a lustre
to Judaism, a dignity to our name, and an honour to our community, of which they have long
been deprived. Even as the evil of deception
spreads little by little, until like a poisonous weed
it covers and deteriorates the whole soil around
it, and destroys all that grows beneath its baneful shade; so also, happily, where truth is planted
and firmly takes root even in a small space, it
grows deeper and stronger and gradually extends
further and further, until, like a mountain pine,
lofty and powerful, its great branches spread wide
and far around, and it remains sole possessor of
the ground it conquered but slowly. We need
wait for none to join us in our great undertaking;
it is a work that can be done single-handed, and
that each man in some measure must do for himself. Clubs, associations, combined forces are
not necessary; we may both commence and carry
on our holy enterprise alone. But it may give us
hope and courage, may animate us with a stronger
zeal and a livelier expectation, to know that our
single efforts in the great cause will be attended
with more than our own individual benefit; they
will surely win over to good and to happiness
some other human heart, and direct some other

human step.   Each man's truth is a beacon to his
fellow pilgrims; its light not only illumines his
own mind, but, shining through it, like the lamp
that burns through the casement of the solitary
lighthouse, it may save many a life from shipwreck.

Let us each in our several spheres of society
make truth our own, beginning not to-morrow but
to-day, beginning with prayer and faith, beginning with an upright will and solemn intent, and
the God who beholds and watches over us will bless
our efforts, will make us see more and more clearly
His will, hear more and more distinctly His voice,
understand more and more fully His law, until in
love, in peace, and holiness we shall manifest in
ourselves, and see realised in others, God's
Eternal Truth.

CHAPTER III.

THE LABOURER'S SABBATH.

You have had a week of toil, hard toil, shut up in close rooms; your hands have ached from plying the needle or holding the heavy tool so long; your eyes are dim and strained from poring over your work from early morning till late at night; and a sense of weariness has stolen over you, from continual application and the imprisonment of a whole week. But now comes the Sabbath, the labourer's blessed Sabbath, and the wearied hand, the wearied eye, and still more wearied mind, may take their rest. The calm peaceful Sabbath is come, to give you the repose and comfort that you so much require.

The evening has closed in, one by one the stars come glimmering out upon the dark sky, the busy sounds of busy day gradually cease till silence is around us, a silence that is so grateful after the harsh and perpetual noise of the stirring

city. Husbands, fathers, bend their steps home-
wards, and wives and children have arranged their
dwellings, put forth their best to-night, and
dressed themselves in their nicest attire, to do
honour to the Sabbath eve. How cheerful an
evening it may be, if honest feelings, if kindly
thoughts, if devotion to God and man, are but
there! How beautiful a light rests upon the
home where dwells the spirit of love! palaces
are dark without it, and the poorest house is light
when love shines upon its hearth.

Have you books, have you a Bible to read to
each other after supper? for a few appropriate
words, a Psalm, or a chapter of the Pentateuch
or Prophets, is such a good welcome to the Sabbath, so suitable a commencement for the hallowed evening. Group around your hearth; little
ones and grey-haired parents, strong men and
blithesome matrons, and open the sacred book
that has been our friend and guide, and our
fathers' before us, and let us listen to the Voice
that spoke, three thousand years ago, the words
that fall so soothingly upon our hearts to-night.

It will tell you—and amidst the world's hard-
ships and trials you may sometimes forget it—that
the Creator of heaven and earth, the Supreme
Ruler of the universe, is your God and Father,

that He is with you in your dwellings, with you in the wide world, with you everywhere and evermore. It tells you that your struggles after good, that your patient endurance of evil and sorrow, that your hard life, serenely, bravely borne, is the purest worship that you can offer up to the Divine Being. That ancient Voice, that sounds so sweetly as it comes over the wide dark tract of the past to us,—that Voice will tell you that, however poor and lowly you may be in the eyes of the world, you are great and noble in God's sight. It will tell you that the richest man, who dwells in a gorgeous palace, with the costliest gems around him, has nothing more precious or more glorious than you possess. God's noblest gift has been given to all His children—a mind created in His own image, and destined to live eternally. It will tell you how God loves this immortal mind, and how it has to be trained and perfected for its final home; how good and evil, how sorrow and joy, how poverty and wealth are alternately sent to purify and chasten, to discipline and strengthen our minds and hearts; to make them beautiful and pure, a fitting sanctuary for God's Spirit to abide in. You may have felt inclined during the week's labour to complain of the hardness of your fate, of the ills you have to endure; but they will be forgotten to-night or rather meekly accepted, as coming from a merciful Father, who keeps a faithful watch over His children. The solemn remembrance that you are a child of God; that you have a mind like unto His mind, that you are the creature of His love, will shed a light over your path, and it will seem dark and weary no more. You may have wished for a higher destiny, an easier life, more comforts, more wealth, and more distinction; but these vain yearnings will cease when you remember to-night that, when all these outward things shall have passed away—when all the luxuries and honours of earth shall have crumbled into dust— your mind and spirit will still be living eternally in an everlasting home, in the presence of God for evermore.

Mother, when you bend to-night in prayer over your infant's cradle, the rosy sleeper will be more sacred than ever in your eyes. Your heart will be less anxious and troubled, indeed, for its worldly welfare; but you will have higher and nobler hopes for the child of your love; you will be more content with the earthly lot God has appointed it; but you will strive more zealously to make that young mind pure, and good, and true, worthy of its God and Father.

Young girl, the dictates of vanity, the whispers

of pride, that perhaps have haunted you during the week, will be stilled to-night; only the solemn Voice, calling upon you to be true to God and yourself, will be heard.

Old man, who standest upon the very verge of this life, worn and weary with its long struggles, thy heart will feel young to-night, young with the blessed hope of immortality. To thee this Sabbath will seem a type, a promise of the eternal sabbath that awaits those that love and serve their God, and thy slumbers will be calm and happy, even as the cradled child's, who has known in its little life no care or grief, no labour, and no misery. Above you and above us all shineth God's heaven, and above that and above us all is His mercy and His love that filleth all time and all space. Sleep, sleep, wearied ones of earth, He keeps a vigil over you, you are safe in His holy keeping.

Now rises the Sabbath morn. The sun salutes the earth with its roseate beams, and penetrates into streets and alleys, into huge dark buildings, into old grey edifices, beneath arches and portals, giving to all things a look of cheerfulness and renovated life wherewith to welcome day.

I wish you could see the morning break, not as it does here, over tall houses, and gables, and spires, through a dense atmosphere with which it seems to battle, but see it break over hill and dale, enveloping with its rays all things in a flood of light. I wish you could breathe the morning air, not through a narrow casement as it steals adown your courts and streets, but breathe it in the fine open country, as it comes like a gushing stream laden with the freshness of green fields, with the fragrance of flowers, with the scent of new-made hay, or, better still, as it comes from the snowy mountains or the joyous sea. I wish you could wander forth into lanes and meadows, under the shade of wood and copse, amidst early primroses and violets, and listen there to the joyous yet solemn matin hymn offered up by nature to nature's God.

I wish, but it is an idle wish, for we are shut up in close streets and dingy places, and no fields with their new-mowed grass, no sequestered lanes with their hedges of wild roses and creepers, no fine old trees with mossy seat beneath their pendant branches, invite you forth to-day, or lead you by their gentle beauty to thought and prayer.

It is one of the saddest features of our present position that our life is chiefly passed in the warfare and the confinement of great cities, and that spring and summer pass away, year after

year, without our feeling their beauty or their
gladness.　Children of Israel, it was not always
thus.　When God delivered our fathers, from bondage and misery, and elected us to be His chosen
people, this was not the life prepared for us,—this
was not the destiny whose rainbow colours arched
over and illumined the wilderness.　The vine-clad
hills of Judea, its murmuring streams with bright
pebbles shining beneath their pellucid waters,
waving palms and lofty cedars, flowers and fruit in
luxurious profusion, birds with bright wings and
silver sound, a cloudless sky and crystal atmosphere,—these rise up in contrast to the Jewish
quarters where our people dwell.　And the Ju-
dean labourer's life !　The tiller of the ground, the
dresser of the vineyard, the harvest reaper, the
fisherman with his nets by the bright blue sea,
the homestead on the hills or cot in the sheltered
valley, with busy matrons at their home duties:
these rise up before me, and by their side, grim
and gaunt, stands another picture, the clothesman
with his dusty bag, the street dealer with his heavy
tray of portable goods, the pale sempstress in her
back attic, hundreds and hundreds of poor, of
old and young, pent up betwixt grey walls, longing for more air and more light.

But, even as we are, let us welcome our sabbath, dismiss sadness and painful recollections, and welcome our day of leisure and repose, our day of peace and home enjoyment, of prayer and worship, of holy thought and holy feeling.

Clothesman, lay down your dusty bag. Dealer, put by your wares. Sempstress, place those heavy garments on one side ; and labourers give up your weary business, and welcome your sabbath. Your minds may be free to-day, free to devote themselves to a moral and spiritual life, to the true, to the good, to the eternal. You are free to-day, free to be with your families, to teach your little ones to know and serve their God, to give pleasure to those around you, to think of better things than the weekly toil and drudgery : you are free to go to the house of prayer, and together with your brethren offer up praise and song to God. Welcome your sabbaths—they are the noblest institutions that Time has handed down to us, and through us to the whole civilised world. The spirit of our sabbath rests, in some measure, upon the Christian Sunday, and to that day of repose and devotion our happy England owes in part its piety and its prosperity. When you hear the church bell or village chime, and see throngs of people bending their way from palace and from cottage to the house of prayer,

you may feel a happy pride, that to us our
Christian brethren owe one of their greatest
blessings.

In times of persecution and sore trials,
amidst danger and flight, in exile and in prison,
our fathers consecrated God's holy day; and now
that we live in security and peace, let nothing
induce us to violate the solemn ordinance that is
enjoined so emphatically and lovingly throughout
the Bible. " Thou shalt remember the Sabbath-
day to keep it holy," was a commandment proclaimed in the name of God to the whole house
of Israel, and it was to be an everlasting covenant between the Almighty Father and His
children.

Blessings many and great were attached to
its observance; chastisements heavy and severe
to its violation. God knew how necessary such
a day is to man, and He appointed it to be a
stronghold for their virtue, a repose from the
world's warfare, a season of retirement and calm,
a sanctuary where no petty cares, no troubles, no
thought of labour, no worldly passion, or selfish
ambition should intrude. If such a day was
needed by the Israelites in their free and joyous
land, amidst the smiles of a beautiful landscape
and sunny sky, where they pursued, prince or

soldier, chief or peasant, honoured and pleasant
vocations ; how much more do we, whose position
is so sadly different, need its solace ? and how
much more must we, who are deprived of earthly
blessings, require the spiritual good that the
Sabbath confers ?   They, the happier ones, require the day to teach them how to use their
prosperity wisely—teach them how to remain true
to God, amidst honour and joy, amidst freedom
and fortune.   We require it to teach us to use
adversity aright, to give us strength to endure,
to battle, and to conquer; to lead us, who have
strayed so far away, back to God, to a true piety,
to a pure religion, to holy thoughts and holy
actions.

We require the day to search our inmost
hearts, and see their inner faults, not the sins
only that our fellow-man observes, but those
frailties that we and God can alone detect, from
within the secrecy of their close shelter.

We have to bring our virtues also to the light
of Heaven, and see if they are real or but the
shadows, the semblance of virtues dressed up in
artificial colours and array.   We must read the
record of the week as it stands registered in our
minds (it is registered in God's book also), and
see what progress towards good we have made,

G

or what downward steps we have taken : we have
all a rough tract to pass; we have all a steep
hill to climb; have we gained in the ascent, or
have we lost what way we made the week before?

How fares it with us, not with our worldly
fortune, but with the treasures confided to us by
the Almighty God, and of which we shall have to
render a solemn account ?   Have we improved or
increased them, or do they lie idle and waste in
our possession ?   Take advantage of the pause the
world makes around you to-day to ask yourselves
these questions, and listen to the answer that
the mind and heart alone can make.   See how
the moral ledger stands, what profit and what
loss, what balance its pages mark.

The day is not far distant, for any of us, when
that ledger shall be opened and read under the
radiant light of Eternity, when all its secrets
shall be disclosed and judgment passed upon it.
Wait not, wait not for that awful day, that
eternal Sabbath, to cast up your account.   Be
it our weekly task, a holy Sabbath duty.   It will
lead us to God, lead us repentantly and humbly
as a contrite child to its father, and as a father
God will receive the confession and accept the
repentance.   All outward worship, all rites, all
ceremonies will be useless, until we know our-

selves, our passions and our weakness, our frailties and our sins, and are prepared to struggle with them, to root them from out our hearts, to sacrifice all things that shall stand betwixt us and our moral welfare, between us and God.

Welcome your Sabbaths, they give you the leisure you need to attend to life's noblest and truest duties; fathers and mothers, welcome them; they give you the time you need to fulfil your duty to your children, to gather them round you in prayer and in companionship. Make the day joyful to them, be serene, be calm, speak words of cheerfulness and love to the young and joyous, speak holy words that shall dwell in their memories long after they are spoken: when they in their turn shall have grown into manhood and have little ones standing at their knees, they shall remember their early home Sabbaths; and they shall bless that father or that mother that cultivated their love for God, and gave them with that love the only true inheritance, the only incorruptible and eternal good.

Welcome your Sabbath, all ye labourers; welcome it as a token from God that this toiling weary life is not our *all*, but that we are spiritual beings as well as creatures of clay, and that we have not only to care for the mortal

frame, but for the soul—the immortal spirit.
Through all your hard work, through all the
city's noise, through all the harsh cries around,
through the rolling wheels, through the heavy
steps, through the world's anxieties, passions,
and discordance, feel your spirituality, feel
your affinity to the eternal God. Through your
torn, soiled garments, through your miserable
dwellings, through your dark walls, through all
your outward poverty, feel your spiritual greatness, feel that you are the noblest work of God's
creation.

Welcome, welcome your Sabbaths, oh, my
brethren, for they proclaim to us these truths;
they are to us a type, a hope, and a sure covenant.

CHAPTER IV.

THOUGHTS ON THE DAY OF REST.

THE Sabbath is a great name, and a great day, honoured throughout the civilized world, ushered in by solemnities and consecrated by prayer and devotion.

Judaism and Christianity both recognise the Sabbath alike, enjoining its observance, though it is celebrated upon different days.

From every city and hamlet of England the deep-toned cathedral bell or rural chime or swelling strain of pealing organ comes floating upon the tranquil air, summoning a vast nation to the house of worship. Noble streets and narrow alleys, meadow paths and shady lanes, are thronged with young and old, with blithesome children, with gray-haired men, with rich and poor, seeking the house of God, to offer up in unison adoration and thanksgiving.

The traveller pauses on his laborious pilgrimage to celebrate the day of rest and seek out God's altars, a home for the spiritual being, beneath whatever clime those altars rise. The hardy mariner suspends his labour to consecrate upon the wide seas the Sabbath-morn, and the voice of prayer mingles with the music of the waves.

Wherever the Bible has left its track of light upon distant shores, where palms and cedars wave; in ice-bound lands, where polar stars gleam bright by day; in far-off isles, where the deep surge beats against a lonely beach, the Sabbath is solemnized, not in synagogue, or church, or beneath cathedral dome alone, but upon the free sea-shore, upon mountain heights, under the spreading sail and waving flag, amid the smiles of nature, beneath the broad arch of heaven, in God's own bright and beautiful universe.

Within prison walls the Sabbath dawns with a holy light. The condemned of man hears upon that day the voice of divine mercy calling upon the fallen, though still the child of God, to return to the Almighty Father, and many a redeemed mind may trace its recovered virtue to the Sabbath's blessed ministry. In the sad but beneficent hospital the moan of pain is hushed for a time to welcome the Sabbath. The

words of peace, spoken from out God's holy book,
have healing in their sound; and most precious
are its immortal hopes, that kindle a fresh power
and awaken a spiritual life, that may grow
stronger and brighter even as the physical life
declines and fades away.

Images of peace and sanctity, drawn from out
memory's old cells, group themselves in beautiful
though shadowy array, around the day of rest.
Childhood's happy home, the household met in
prayer, the father's blessing, the bible stories told
by twilight round the mother's knee, the walk
amid green fields and primrose woods, over which
a solemn light was shed by solemn thought;
these memories, still fresh and pure as sabbath
treasures once enjoyed and loved so well, come
clustering round many a heart.

For us unhappily, as with all our festive and
hallowed days, our Sabbath is no longer ushered
in by a universal consecration; whilst we so-
lemnize our day of rest, the labour, the revelry,
and the warfare of the busy world go on.

We are not surrounded upon our Sabbath, as
Christians are, by a religious atmosphere,—no solemn sounds fall upon the ear—no holy melody fills
the air—no groups upon groups wending their
way to the house of worship meet our eye, but

we hear only the harsh voice of the city's ceaseless toil, we see only striving, careworn, anxious,
or restless faces, human beings carrying on the
world's warfare and labour.

There is inspiration in the example of a multitude, and this inspiration is wanting to us. In
the enthusiasm of the many there is something
contagious, and of this enthusiasm we are deprived. To this cause may, in part, be attributed
the frequent desecration of the Sabbath amongst
us. The ledger and the needle are laid aside ; the
warehouse is closed and the exchange is deserted ;
but still, amongst many, nothing holy or solemn
takes the place of their weekly avocations. The
world around us is intent upon business or pleasure, and we cannot exclude ourselves from the
world. Open shops, galleries, exhibitions, public
places of resort, are constant allurements, and
help to fill up the weariness of an empty day.
It cannot be disguised we have many and great
temptations to violate the Sabbath ; a faithful
adherence to its laws must at times call forth a
sacrifice on our part, a heavy sacrifice to the industrial class. It must be said to the honour of
our poor, that they often resist temptation more
successfully than their more prosperous brethren.

In many a lowly Jewish home the poor forego

the pittance they might earn—the little pittance needed to eke out a scanty livelihood—to their sense of duty, to their love of God. They celebrate in peace and thankfulness their calm Sabbath, even whilst Poverty, pale and attenuated, crouches beside their hearth. And they have their recompense, for in their triumph over temptation, in their obedience and self-denial, a moral strength and dignity is gained, which is the best guardian of the poor—the surest barrier between themselves and sin.

It is a painful reflection that the Sabbath is chiefly desecrated by those upon whom its observance would entail no privation but that of worldly pleasures, no restraint but from frivolous pursuits, and would offer no obstacle but to an unhallowed ambition and an insatiable love of gain. There are many who would not publicly profane the day of rest, but who, contenting themselves with an outward decorum, attach no idea of sanctity, no religious feeling to its observance; and this superficial and hollow respect—a homage paid to the world—only becomes a mockery or a subterfuge in the sight of God. The evil, unhappily, is not confined to a limited class, for as the position and education of the wealthiest members of society make them the example of the

community, so there are many in an humbler
sphere of life who violate the Sabbath from the
habit of imitation, and from the love of following in the footsteps of more opulent men
than themselves. But for all classes it is the
same Sabbath ; and whilst all have temptations to
desecrate its rest and its holiness, we all have the
strongest and most solemn inducements to hallow
the day that was equally committed to the
guardianship of all Israel.

It is for all alike the Sabbath, that was proclaimed by the Eternal God, amidst the thunders
of Sinai, to the whole Jewish nation; that was
given as an everlasting inheritance, to be bequeathed from age to age, from generation to
generation, as a link and a covenant between
the Almighty Father and His redeemed people.

" Remember the sabbath-day to keep it holy,"
said the Eternal Voice. " Six days shalt thou
labour and do all thy work : but the seventh day
is the sabbath of the Lord thy God : in it thou
shalt not do any work, thou, nor thy son, nor thy
daughter, thy man-servant, nor thy maid-servant,
nor thy cattle, nor the stranger that is within thy
gates."

In every house of prayer that is dedicated to
the Supreme Being, we find this commandment

inscribed upon its altars ; we find it in its liturgy, and accepted as universal and eternal.

Throughout the Bible we find the consecration of the Sabbath to holiness and to God again and again enforced upon the house of Israel; we find this hallowed day delineated with a gentle beauty in the Psalmist's songs of praise and worship, and emphatically recommended as a stringent law in the sterner language of the Prophets.

The voice of ages comes clear and distinct from distant shores proclaiming the mission of the Sabbath, and it becomes us to listen to the voice that, journeying on from shore to shore, has still spoken the same words and reiterated the same injunctions. In tracing back these records we find that the Sabbath was consecrated by the suffering race who had just passed from bondage to liberty. "Thou shalt labour but six days, then take thy rest," must have been a welcome command, contrasting happily, indeed, with the ceaseless toil and the galling servitude whose bitterness was yet a living memory. In the desert, with danger and privation still around them, prayers of deep thanksgiving must have been offered up for the day of rest which bespoke them free men at last. And when their time of probation was passed, and they took possession

of the land which was to be a peaceful home to
the passing generation and a fatherland to their
children, a hallowed greeting must have been
given to the Sabbath-day which proclaimed to
them each successive week their existence as a
free people, whose moral and spiritual welfare was
henceforth to be a first and sacred interest; not
all physical labour, not all toil and degradation,
not all worldly gain and worldly gratification, but
in each Jewish home was to be solemnized, by
rich and poor, by servants and by strangers, by
the noblest and the lowliest of the land, a day of
intellectual and moral freedom, a day of thought
and prayer, of holy communion with the God
and Father of all mankind. Joyously must the
husbandman with his family around him have
reposed from his weekly toil, and beneath the
spreading trees of his own planting have taught
his children to know and serve their God.

In those peaceful homes the history of the
past was related, the slavery of their fathers,
their glad deliverance, Moses' great and holy
mission, the revelation on Mount Sinai, which
brought them moral light and moral freedom.
And the evening breeze must have come soft
and refreshingly across the blue hills that encircled their city, and the stars have taken their

watch in the deep ether above them, whilst still they listened to that solemn history, and learnt their glorious destiny, their task on earth, and the immortal hopes that painted another land and home in colours even brighter than their present one.

Prepared by a day of rest and of prayer, of communion with the beautiful, the true and holy, passed amid nature's loveliest scene, the morrow's sun must have risen upon men strengthened to fulfil life's toils and duties—fulfil them with the mind and heart, nobly and truthfully, as well as with the hand and body.

One loves to linger amid those early days, amid a free people, who led a simple but dignified existence under the government of God, the Almighty and Eternal, who was their King, their Redeemer, and Father.

One loves to linger amidst those pure calm Sabbaths which realized the good and happiness which they were destined to confer; but short is the time comprising those happy annals, and we soon reach darker days and desolate epochs.

Interwoven still with the history of the house of Israel we find the Sabbath honoured in its days of religion and happiness, desecrated and neglected in its sadder epochs, when its homes its palaces, and temple had lost what constituted their glory, a truthful piety and a pure worship. What solemn remonstrances were addressed to the nation by the voice of inspiration! what pathetic pleadings in favour of the Sabbath!—but vain were the remonstrances, and vain the pleadings; the Sabbath was still profaned, and with its profanation came the downfall of the Jewish nation. The minds and hearts that could not pause amidst their earthly labours and exactions, amidst their worldly vanities and pomps, to give a welcome to the day of freedom, to pass a few hours in repose, in prayer and worship, were in themselves too ignoble or too enervated, too mercenary or too depressed, too much the slaves of the world, to be faithful guardians of their own prosperity and welfare.

The Sabbath's calm and liberty, the few hours it bestowed for communion with the solemn and divine, with the beautiful and the eternal, was the best safeguard Judea possessed.

It had girt her sons with power and virtue, it had endowed her daughters with purity and faith, and in their spiritual and moral greatness she was safe and prosperous. This moral greatness once departed, she became defenceless. Her impregnable forts and citadels, her proud armies and princes, her sea-girt coast and mountain heights availed her no longer. She fell in spite of all the protection with which art and nature had surrounded her, not from the oppressive hand without her gates, not beneath the force of foreign might, but from the tyranny and the weakness, from the degradation and the sin, that darkened her homes, that ruled her hearths and cradled her young.

Then came centuries of misery, and grief, and trial, God's dispensation to a faithless nation.

A reaction took place in the minds of the people; in their fallen state they attached a supreme value and importance to the ordinances they had neglected or despised in their halcyon days. Adversity made them cling with a strange pertinacy to the ceremonies of the Mosaic Law; but unfortunately, as outward forms and observances grew dearer and dearer to them, the spiritual faith and precepts of Judaism became less and less the governing principle of their minds, until at length they no longer constituted the great basis or formed predominant features of their religion. Teachers arose in numbers, but they encouraged their disciples to a puerile observance of Judaism; whilst they themselves devoted years of earnest labour to the unravelling of

sophistical enigmas and arguments, and in add-
ing a burthensome ritual to a law that was clear
and beautiful in its original simplicity and grandeur.

It must, however, be a subject more of surprise
and gratulation that Judaism was preserved at all,
than that she should not have passed unsullied
through those desolate ages, when superstition
and bigotry threw a moral blight over the whole
earth, destroying the bloom and beauty of all
religion. Throughout all vicissitudes that have
no parallel in history, the Sabbath was still preserved, and it would be no uninteresting task to
trace its ministry through these desolating epochs.
It was not, perhaps, hallowed any longer as the
solemn and spiritual day that God had destined
as a blessing and a joy to His emancipated children, that was to lead a holy nation and a kingdom
of priests even nearer and nearer to the eternal
throne; but still, amidst peril and sorrow, amidst
persecution and death, the day of rest was celebrated. In Spain and Portugal, where a public
profession of Judaism was punished by exile or
death, the Sabbath was still observed. In the
secrecy of apartments so dextrously contrived
that they were ignored to the household at large,
the sabbath lamps were lighted, the festive table

prepared, wives and mothers, husbands and fathers, gray-haired men and rosy children, assembled in the secluded chambers, and Sabbath hymns were lowly chaunted and Sabbath prayers were offered up to God, with loud-beating hearts, but whispered voices.

Stronger than the fear of discovery, stronger than the dread of exile or of death, stronger than the affection which links kindred hearts together, which knits husband and wife, child and parent, in the closest bonds, was their love of God, was their obedience to His commandments.

These whispered prayers of heroic hearts and souls must have risen as upon angels' wings to God.

Thus the Jewish Sabbath has passed from age to age, from land to land; now, as our hapless race enjoyed liberty of conscience and a temporary cessation from persecution, it was openly celebrated in our synagogues and our homes; and then again, when intolerance and bigotry woke up with a renewed and vindictive zeal, it was observed in secrecy and in silence; but amidst all changes of country and of position, amidst sudden flights and long wanderings, upon the shores of a dreary exile, in the dungeon of the Inquisition, the Sabbath was remembered still.

H

And thus it has at last reached our times, having
retained its great office and sacred character;
but, like all things borne to us adown the stream
of Time, it has come in some measure with the
soils and impurities of life's troubled current
clinging round it, weeds that attach themselves
to the surface of the gem, but that cannot penetrate its substance.

This is an age of extremes—of grave orthodoxy
and of scoffing infidelity, of complete indifference
and of perplexing doubt. We partake of the
characteristics of the age in which we live, and
Judaism has more faces than Janus possessed of
old.

In looking round us we find a few who carry
out with a Puritan severity the minute forms and
laws with which the Rabbinical teachers have
invested the Sabbath. Then there is a class who
affect a respect they do not feel, and observe
the day of rest as a deference paid to public
opinion, to the religious feeling of the country
in which we live. Then there are others who,
more indifferent to the world's estimation, or
possessed of bolder minds, discard all religious
observances, and with these discard the Sabbath
as a useless appendage of the past. There are a
few amongst us who, with a deep religious feeling,

seek to further their moral progress, and who, as a means of spiritual good, and of communion with the divine and holy, enshrine in their minds' sanctuary the Sabbath day.

These, however, form the limited exception; and now in England, where we have full liberty to worship the God of our fathers according to the dictates of our conscience, where in happy security we may seek the house of prayer dedicated to the one infinite God only, and in calm and peace we may celebrate the Sabbath of the Bible, we too often desecrate our faith, our worship, and our day of freedom; profane them by a bigoted or an unspiritual observance, by the love or fear of the world, or by frivolous pursuits, or the sordid calculations of a poor ambition.

As long as we profess Judaism, as long as we do not openly repudiate her laws, the Sabbath has a solemn claim upon us. It is not for us as Jews to treat with indifference and contempt an institution derived from Judaism, whose salutary influence has been acknowledged by the civilized world, which has so widely tended to humanize, and purify, and diffuse a deep religious principle in the human mind.

It is not for us, the descendants of martyrs, to pass lightly over the day for which our fathers perilled their lives, and celebrated as a blessing and a hope amidst darkness, persecution, and death.

And, most of all, it is not for us, as long as we recognise the divine authority of the Bible, to desecrate the day that it holds as sacred, that the Eternal Voice proclaimed as a perpetual covenant between Himself and the children of Israel.

It is not a blind homage or a blind acceptance, however, that we owe the Sabbath; but we are called upon to investigate its mission and its rights, and see whether we can give it our mind's full welcome, our judgment's full assent, and realize it in truth within ourselves: all other observance is futile, or worse than futile—a pretence or a mockery.

Some minds may hesitate to receive the Sabbath, or realize in themselves its mission as being an institution of the past. They see that much that belonged to other lands and times has necessarily undergone considerable change, and that in many instances tradition has handed down to us the records of antiquity in so imperfect a state, that we fail to recognise in their altered character what once perhaps was beautiful and holy in them.

To these minds—philosophical, though doubting—serious, though mistrustful—it may be said, in something more faithful than the page of history, in something more stable than the monuments of the past, the Sabbath is preserved, and evidence is found of its being destined to outlive other institutions that may be destroyed or marred by time.

These proofs are not preserved upon marble, traced in hieroglyphic characters, or in dim records of twilight ages, but we find them inscribed upon the human soul. The Sabbath has an existence in the mind itself, and owes its birth to the wants and to the capacities of our moral nature.

Thus cities may rise and fall, thus creeds may be established and sink into insignificance, but still the Sabbath would remain, for the human mind, greater far than cities and creeds, gives it a sanctuary in its temple; and there it dwells, the friend, the monitor, the blessing of the home it guards and purifies.

It lives not, therefore, more in the past than in the present; therefore it is not a memorial of

gone-by ages and worn-out customs, it is not an
alien that wears a foreign garb or speaks a foreign language, but it belongs to all ages, all
climes, all people, and speaks to us in familiar
and living words. It addresses itself not to a
particular race only, dwelling apart from their
fellow-men, but to the universal family, to the
child of God, to the spiritual being whose inner
revelations and spiritual truths must remain un-
changed as long as holiness, as heaven, and as
God remain eternal.

We are all conscious of the mind's affinity to
the Supreme Being, we are sensible of its unfathomable thoughts, its lofty aspirations, and its
bright-winged hopes, but yet the spiritual life
which embodies these hopes and thoughts is not
the one we habitually lead. Beside and around
us is the world, with its labours and its cares, its
pomps and its vanities; before us is virtue, is
duty, is eternity; the Sabbath is a bridge thrown
across life's troubled waters, over which we may
pass to reach the opposite shore—a link between
earth and heaven.

Six days' toil and care, six days' worldly avocations and pursuits, and then a pause, a solemn
pause, and in the deep quiet that falls upon the
outward world the inner voice may be heard

speaking to the inner being. The merchant and
the labourer, the peasant and the prince, the
artist and the mechanic may lay aside their outward professions to assume their primitive distinctions and their noblest title, that of spiritual
beings.

Tools, implements, ledgers, pen, pencil, sword
and sceptre may be laid down to take up life's
nobler treasures and holier weapons, drawn from
the great storehouse, where all may go—no first,
no last—and whence all may derive strength, and
hope, and peace.

And there at that great storehouse man meets
his fellow-man, not as a harsh competitor for
earthly honours, not as a contending rival for
earth's distinctions, not as creditor and debtor,
not as different classes who have no fellowship
together, not as rich and poor, prosperous and
unfortunate, but as beings formed and endowed
alike — as the children of one Almighty Father, as brethren treading with pilgrim staff the
same pathway, and as humble worshippers in the
same temple, God's universal house of prayer,
whose altars are raised in every land, and whose
pealing anthems fill all nature.

Beautiful is the Sabbath's ministry, addressing
itself to all that is permanent and holy in the

human heart, a good offered to all, in right
of the mind which requires it, and to which it
gives an existence itself independent of time and
place.

It is a day of rest that the spiritual being may
pass more immediately in his Father's presence;
it is a day of freedom, in which thought and
hope, unfettered by earthly chains, may soar
upward and upward into eternity and happiness.
It is a day when, at peace with ourselves and
mankind, we may join our voice to the voice of
millions in prayer and thanksgiving.

It is the poor man's right and comfort, the
rich man's help; bringing repose and liberty to
the toiling child of earth, truer feelings and
calmer influences to the pampered child of fortune, inspiring both with nobler aspirations and
hopes, freeing the one perhaps for a time from
depressing cares and toils, the other from idle
vanities and selfish passions, imparting to both
the same solemn truths, reminding both that
they are journeying on towards the same home,
where an eternal Sabbath awaits them.   For
as the earthly Sabbath calls upon the worldly
being to give place to the spiritual one, to lay
aside for awhile the cares and labours of earth, to
put on the repose and the holiness of heaven, so

it is but a type of the eternal day when the freed spirit, if true to itself and to God, shall put on for ever its robe of immortal holiness and joy.

Such a day, in its calm and purity, in its freedom and happiness, is needed by men of all classes.

It is needed by fathers who in their weekly labours are much and necessarily absent from home, and separated from their family. They require the Sabbath's leisure hours to draw near in familiar thought and kind companionship to their children, to study their characters, to cultivate their affections, and develope the religious sentiment within them. The sweet fellowship of prayer, the interchange of thought, the quiet walk, the common aim and hope, are all required year after year, week after week, to strengthen and to hallow the bond that should exist between father and child.

Our children are often from their earliest infancy abandoned to the care of menials, their moral and religious training left to the work of chance, or confided to those whose religious opinions differ from our own; and yet we expect, when their education is completed, that a warm and strong love for ourselves, and a true devotion

for their early faith, shall animate their hearts
and enable them to withstand the world's trials
and temptations. A fallacious doctrine and hope,
as many a disappointed parent has learnt through
his children's estrangement from himself, or their
renouncement of their father's faith, or of the
precepts that ennoble that faith. The disappointment and grief on the one side, the wrong
on the other, are too often the parents' early
error, their neglect of the child whilst deep
thoughts and conflicting passions were developing themselves in the young mind and
heart.

We may early train a delicate plant into beauty,
we may twine its youthful tendrils round the
strong tree, and thus give it strength and support; but if the work be left until the plant has
attained a more matured growth, it will then
resist our endeavours at culture, and when un-
protected by the firm tree, when the storm comes
it will bend beneath it, or lie altogether uprooted
by the fierce winter's blast.

Thus it is with our children: we must early
commence the work of culture if we would have
it prosper. We must early teach the young mind
to cling to religion as a support and hope, if we
would have that religion a shelter and a safe-guard

to them in after years.   In every home where the
voice of childhood—blithe, happy childhood—
sounds, the celebration of the Sabbath should be a
sacred interest, for it comes to us as a means and a
help to accomplish our first and dearest duties—a
parent's holiest task—the education of his child's
mind and heart.   In after years there will be
joy or grief, peace or disunion, love or estrangement in those homes, in proportion as their Sabbaths have been solemnized in a holy and enlightened spirit.

Again, the Sabbath is needed by man, whatever his vocation may be; for in the turmoil of
the world, in the hurry and bustle of human life,
in the absorbing claims of business, and in the
interest of professional duties from which we
derive emolument, honour, and fame, there is but
little leisure for quiet thought beyond what the
advancement of these pursuits calls forth; long
years may be passed in heavy toil, and age steal
on with its failing strength, without time having
been found for any care or thought of that inner
self which must outlive the outward being for
which we are so eagerly striving to amass treasures, to weave gay robes, to purchase comforts
and honours ;—treasures that are but an earthly
and a transient possession, robes that crumble into

dust, comforts and luxuries that sink into insignificance when the summons comes for us to make ready and appear before our God. We require to know ourselves, and the world does not give us this knowledge.

If poor and lowly, the world treats us with indifference or contempt, and by degrees we estimate ourselves at the world's opinion. We look as those around us look, at our poor attire, at our humble dwellings, and lose sight of the inner being. Beneath tattered garments and bare walls we forget the mind's nobility, its affinity to the Eternal Father, its glorious mission on earth, and its immortal hopes. We see what constitutes our poverty, but we fail to see what constitutes our real greatness.

If rich and prosperous, then the world smiles upon us, and pays us a deferential homage, and we gradually estimate ourselves with great complacency, and take our outward state as a standard of our moral excellence.

In both cases the inner being is lost sight of, and the calm Sabbath, its free hours, its opportunity for self-examination and for communion with the immutable, the holy, and the pure, comes to us as a blessing to restore us to a sense of the true and great, to awaken us to a vivid perception of the treasures that lie beneath the surface, which may be dark or bright, fair or unsightly, but beneath which outward covering is the noblest work of God's creation, a human heart and a human soul.

Those who can realize this truth will learn to estimate themselves aright, for they will feel that neither the world's honours nor its neglect, that neither wealth nor penury, that neither pomp and state nor lowliness, can confer either a true greatness or a real degradation, that these are alone derived from the moral nobleness or the moral deformity of the spiritual being.

These are convictions requisite to all who would tread with serenity and meekness, with truth and courage, life's chequered pathway—to all who would attain an abiding honour and an imperishable happiness. Each well-spent Sabbath brings this conviction, with a fresh power and a stronger life to our minds, and we carry it with us amid our weekly labours as a friend and protector.

Again, the Sabbath's gentle ministry is needed by the lonely, by those whose homes are uncheered by the sympathy of love and the voice of happy youth. They are the few, but they are those perhaps that most require the Sabbath's

holy offices. In the interchange of affection, in
the caresses of children, in the anxieties and fears
that their welfare excites, the native though perhaps uncultured sentiment of religion is awakened.
For the loved and helpless God the Father is implored ; for the helpmate and friend that blesses
our fireside generous thoughts are entertained
and devoted actions are performed ; but for the
lonely there is no gush of tenderness that passes
instinctively into prayer, there are no smiles and
tears that inspire disinterested and self-denying
deeds.

To these, earth's lonely ones, the Sabbath comes
to bring a holy peace. It comes to lead them
with a gentle voice and gentle hand to God's
temple, to unite them in prayer and in devotion
to God's children, to bid them feel themselves
one of His great family, one of a vast but indissoluble brotherhood. It leads them to communion with the Divine mind, to communion with
the great and beautiful, with the pure and eternal ;
and the aspirations of the desolate mind are
satisfied, the solitude of the lonely heart is
gone, the silence of the lonely home is broken,
for love and hope and holiness are there, filling
the mind with unalterable peace and joy. And
then, though no kindred ties are there to bless,

no words of tenderness to cheer, a spirit of love
for mankind, for God's children, a generous disinterested love is aroused, that gives birth to
noble thoughts and virtuous actions.

Blessed is the Sabbath's mission to these, the
little prized, who tread life's shaded paths; and
many a hymn of joy ascends from earth to
heaven, from hearts once weary and desolate,
now consoled and strengthened through its influence—hearts that once were sterile, but that
now bear flowers and fruit, whose bloom and
beauty are not for earth only, but for eternity.

And many more might be cited upon whom
the day of rest exercises a happy ministry, upon
blithesome youth, upon intellectual manhood,
upon toiling mothers, upon weary age, upon all
who have great duties to perform, homes to bless,
minds to enlighten, souls to spiritualize—the
great task that belongs to all, the sublime vocation that is to prepare us for immortality.

Like all noble things, this day's good has to be
sought for and earnestly cultivated. It does not
flash upon us like a meteoric ray, but as sunlight
dawns gradually upon the earth so it dawns upon
the mind, and grows more and more radiant as
we advance into more perfect day. It is the
work of time, of prayer, of the consecration of

the mind to duty and to God; it is the work of earnest self-culture and self-discipline; it is the development of the spiritual being within us. And this culture, this work, and this discipline we may at last, thank God, undertake. In this our free and enlightened country we experience protection from its laws, and tolerance and kindness from the hands of our Christian brethren. We are now free to devote ourselves to the work of our moral and of our intellectual progress. We have no longer task-masters appointing us degrading labours; we have no longer oppressors to obey at the expense of virtue; we have no impending fears to make moral cowards of us, and no persecutions to avert at the expense of virtue and duty. Liberal professions, noble and intellectual vocations, are open to us; a wide and glorious sphere of labour and of duty extends itself before us.

The prison walls that so long inclosed the moral being within a tainted atmosphere and a restricted space are thrown down, and the long-imprisoned mind is free at last to inhale the breath of liberty, and to take its noblest flights and exercise its noblest capacities.

Let us not be like the poor prisoner of the Bastile, who, on being restored to freedom after many years of a desolate seclusion, preferred his dark and narrow cell to the blaze of day, and to the wide but unfamiliar world before him.

Let us not shrink from entering upon a new arena, and from acquiring the qualities that will fit us worthily to perform our part in a wider and a nobler sphere. As constancy and endurance, as fortitude and patience were the virtues of an age of persecution, so truth and purity, so tolerance, so love and mercy are the qualities with which alone we can hope to discharge the duties of the present age.

God, in giving us the Sabbath, the freeman's day, gives us a great opportunity and means of keeping pace with the moral and spiritual progress around us—gives us time for self-knowledge and discipline, for acquiring broad and enlightened views, for a calm study of ourselves and the world.

To realize this good, so important at this moment to us, it must not be viewed as a mere ceremony, as a memorial of the past, or as a formal law imposed upon us, but as a day marked in the mind's calendar to be solemnized by the mind.

The day whose mission is proclaimed by the Bible and by the voice of the divinity within us

I

needsno stern sentinel, no old superstitions, to protect it. Its best guardians are holy thoughts and
solemn feelings, the mind's reverence and welcome.

To some extent each individual must shape
out his own Sabbath, for it should realize a good
to himself, and must therefore harmonize with
the general tone of his mind. When this is not
the case, it becomes an outward, not an inward
solemnity; a day spent for the world, and not
for ourselves; for neither its repose nor its duties,
neither its worship nor its prayers, come home to
our feelings.   Still there is a general outline that
must be preserved, though it has to be filled up
in accordance with individual circumstances and
feeling.

Thus for all it is a day to be consecrated to
holiness; therefore it is incumbent upon all,
whilst they lay aside their worldly avocations and
implements, to lay aside their worldly passions
and their strifes. It is a mockery to God to
put on a garb of sanctity, to attend the house of
prayer with solemn mien and bended knee, and
yet leave mind and heart covered with the soil
and dust of earth. It is a mockery to approach
God's altar without bringing any offering of
virtue, of duty, of humility, and of truth; for
these are now the Sabbath offerings and the

sacrifices that the Almighty Father requires and accepts from His children.

For all it is a day to be consecrated to God, passed more immediately in His presence; it should therefore be made attractive to ourselves and those around us. It should have no dull and weary hours, and for this end it must not be composed of one unvarying round of the same forms that grow by repetition into distasteful monotony. We must each successive week bring to its shrine thoughts and pursuits that will invest it with more interest and power. Fresh and blooming flowers should be gathered every Sabbath morn wherewith to deck its altars.

For all it is to be a day of repose, but not of idleness; a day of physical rest and moral freedom, but not of intellectual or moral inactivity. We derive our spiritual example from nature and from God, and the Divine beneficence, mercy, and love know no time of slumber, but are for ever working on around and within us. And thus our mental and moral faculties are to be exercised upon the Sabbath, upon all our days on earth. There are holy fields for Sabbath labours, where love is sown and love is reaped. There are the homes of the weary and suffering to be visited; there are words of peace and hope to be spoken; there is sympathy and care to be administered to those who tread with failing steps life's rugged pathway; there are ignorant men and women, poor sisters and brothers, whose neglected minds require training, and awakening to the beauty of religion and to the power of virtue.

With the Bible precepts engraven on our heart we may take with us to desolate homes and darkened minds light and hope and joy upon God's holy day.

For all it is a day that is to be a type of the eternal Sabbath; one, therefore, in which the spiritual life is to stand forth in its own pre-eminence. A day redeemed from bondage, a day of freedom and emancipation for the mind, when we may go forth in liberty into God's universe, and listen freely to the voice of nature, and garner up for ourselves images of beauty and solemn revelations of sacred truths. For God does not inclose His highest teachings in books or mysteries that only the learned can unravel, but His spirit breathes from out all nature, speaking clear words that need no interpreter from man to man. It is a Father's voice that speaks, and that adapts His teachings to His children's power. They have but to open their minds to the Divine ministry, and these lessons reach the inmost depths of the inner being. Freely with trust and hope we may approach the source of all knowledge and good, and seek for ourselves virtue and truth—a virtue that weaves a shining thread through all our thoughts and actions—a truth that, like the pillar of fire that led the Israelites of old to freedom, shall lead us now to a moral and spiritual liberty.

We should, as often as it is possible, on the Sabbath leave the glare and tumult of cities, the busy haunts of men, to seek quiet and sequestered scenes where we may hear, whilst all else is still, the music of Nature's voice; where we may listen to the deep murmur of the tall trees' verdant branches, as they wave their arms to and fro in the morning breeze; to the brook's gentle rippling, or louder song of rushing stream; to the bleating of the browsing herd, the hum of busy insects, the carol of the wood's blithe minstrels—a joyous yet a solemn chant—a deep harmony that in glad summer-time fills glades and woods, and fields and glens,—sounds and songs in unison with Sabbath hymns and Sabbath prayers.

In winter days, when frost and snow detain us by our fireside, books that tell of the glory and

wonders of God's creation should take the place
of our sunny walks.

Nothing will give us such enlightened views,
or extend so widely life's horizon before us, as
the study of the Almighty's works. Nothing will
tend more than a knowledge of Nature's laws and
wonders to spiritualize our minds and develope
the image of the divinity within us. We may
also people our hearths with the works of the
great and gifted of all times and all nations, and
hold a quiet communion with the spirit that lives
in the pages they have bequeathed to posterity.
Taylor, Fenelon, Pascal, Mendelsohn, Channing,
Fichte, Parker, and many more as pure and true,
may be the companions of our Sabbaths; to
these let us add such poets as Cowper, Words-
worth, Longfellow, Elizabeth Browning, and Felicia Hemans, whose words of deep humanity and
holy truth, attuned to music, will awaken chords
of religious feeling which sterner prose often
leaves unmoved.

Again, it is for all a day of self-examination,
when the week's records are to be perused. This
retrospective glance, the weak vain thoughts, the
selfish actions, the harsh words, the intolerant
feelings that pass in review before us, take us

humbly to God. His mercy is implored upon
the past, upon its follies and its frailties; and
upon the good achieved, the progress made, the
conquering discipline, His blessing is earnestly
implored. And for the coming week His love
and protection are supplicated; strength for its
trials and temptations, holiness and faith for the
cares and the joys, the hopes and the disappointments, that await us in the outer and the inner
life.

It is, finally, a day which, leading us to God,
should unite mankind in a holy fellowship. It
is a day which should link human hearts together
in a true brotherhood, making them forget minor
differences, conflicting opinions, and dissensions,
in the common bond and in the common aim
and hope that lead them alike to the house of
prayer, to the same God and Father, to offer up
at the same altar thanks and praise and suppli-
cation upon His holy and His peaceful Sabbath-
day.

This is but a general outline of the Sabbath,
the broad characteristics which should mark the
day of rest and holiness. The outline has to be
filled up, many a beautiful detail to be added, and
many a glowing light to be inserted.

Most of us have portrayed an ideal Sabbath;

and there is a good in these paintings of the mind, for they are true to the inner, if not to the outer life, else we could have no such conception of them, and as by degrees the latter will be brought to harmonize more with the spiritual being, with our better self, so the ideal will become more and more a reality. The aspirations of our brightest moments will become permanent feelings, and the transient holiness that elevates our soul to God will become the fixed principle of our lives.

As by degrees our weekly day of rest is solemnized in holiness and truth, in love and peace, as it is passed in communion with the good and noble, and in the presence of the Almighty God, it will spiritualize our whole life, it will bring Sabbath thoughts and feelings into our every day's avocations, into our business transactions, in our home duties, in our pleasures and our cares. Then all places will be holy, all professions will be ennobled, all occupation will be hallowed, for then the world will be a temple where God will be worshipped in spirit and in truth; not in outward forms or ceremonies, not in synagogue or temple, not on festive or solemn days only, but in the heart and mind, in our daily life and daily actions—the spiritual worship of spiritual beings.

Such is the mission of the Jewish Sabbath ; such the hallowed day bestowed upon the children of Israel.   Let us who profess Judaism fulfil its divinest institution.   Let us who acknowledge the one Supreme God and Infinite Father obey the sublime commandment that was proclaimed by the Eternal Voice.   Let us consecrate God's divine and solemn ordinance to a pure and spiritual worship, to love, to mercy, and to truth ; let us realize the beauty and the good of God's day of moral freedom, of God's day of peace and holiness, of God's eternal Sabbath.

CHAPTER V.

THE PASSOVER.

In this festival we celebrate a great national deliverance, but, yet more, we celebrate the birth of Judaism, we give a solemn welcome to the faith that three thousand years ago, upon this eventful night, struggled into existence, an active life-giving existence.

Armed by the power of a glorious revelation, nerved by the inspiration of divine truths, Moses undertook the greatest mission that man has ever performed. The meek and gentle man, who had been leading so peaceful a life in his pastoral home, amid home-cherished ties, grew strong and heroic, and returned to Egypt to battle with oppression and tyranny, to contend with the weakness of an enslaved people, to whose deliverance he devoted his life. After a long and arduous struggle, the sublime faith within him achieved a mighty conquest over the pride of despotism and over the degradation of slavery

The monarch, subdued by a greater power than his own, consented at last to the departure of the oppressed race from the land where they had laboured in slavery, where they had shed tears of bitter misery, but to which they still clung as to their native soil.

Within their dark Egyptian homes, prepared for the night's solemn event, hastily, with staff in hand and pilgrim attire, the children of Israel eat, for the last time, the bread of a bitter servitude; and then, confiding their destiny to God, they go forth amid the protecting shades of night; manhood and age, trembling women and helpless children, go forth from the shelter of old homes, to the untried and the unknown.

As might have been expected from that long-suffering multitude, they trod the path of the wilderness with failing steps and heavy hearts, and their murmurs broke forth into open rebellion when daylight revealed to their view Egypt's powerful army encamped upon the neighbouring heights. Death seemed around and upon them, death in its most grim and horrid aspect. A smile rested upon the graves of Egypt, where their fathers reposed in peace, but over the dreary desert despair alone brooded with its sable wing. It was horrible, amid this universal desolation, to take a last farewell of husband, wife, and child, and meet the embrace of death. Strong and true must have been the spirit and the faith that sustained their leader, and enabled him to guide them on to life and liberty. Through the parted waves of the Red Sea the despairing multitude pass in safety, and from the sheltering land witness the destruction of the proud army whose attack had seemed inevitable.

Upon the sea-shore, with heaven's light above and heaven's air around them, the slaves of yesterday, the freemen of to-day, paused to salute the dawn and inhale the breath of liberty.

From out free hearts, re-echoed by thousands and thousands of voices, burst a triumphant song—the most solemn and the most rapturous hymn that ever rose from earth to heaven, from man to God.

Let us pause upon the shore of time, and lift up our hearts in thanksgiving and joy for the freedom purchased centuries ago, but which still lives for us, a spiritual and moral freedom that was the gift of the sublime faith that woke into glorious life within the hearts of bondsmen, and grew into beauty and maturity in the wilderness. Misery was its cradle, probation its school; amid varying elements, amid conflict and danger, it acquired strength and power, until at last, triumphing over all things, it reigned a mighty conqueror over human hearts.

Thus ever amid trial and hardship great and permanent things are reared. The flower that blooms in the sheltered garden or hot-house bed, puts forth to-day fair leaves and glowing petals, but to-morrow they lie faded or scentless in our path. The tree that grows upon the mountain side, exposed to storm and wind, looks up to heaven with strong outstretched arms, and receives as a good both the summer's sunshine and the winter's blast.

Thus as a mighty mountain tree embedded deep in earth but ever looking upwards, was Judaism planted in the heart of man, receiving its light and culture from above. Beneath its shelter virtues unknown till then blossomed with an enduring fragrance and beauty. Firmly indeed it grew, for of how many things has it survived the fall! It has witnessed the decline of nations which have buried creed after creed beneath their ruins. The faiths that animated the temples of ancient Greece and Rome lie sepulchred beneath their crumbling columns and their shattered altars.

Not so with Judaism; it has mourned, indeed, over the ruins of its most glorious sanctuaries, but it lives unharmed amid the decay of earthly monuments. The brightness of eastern skies, the smiles of sunny climes, are not essential to its existence.

The spirit of Judaism is universal, independent of time or place, and in every land and in every age it may have a consecrated home, and temple, and altars upon which kindling flames and worship may ascend to heaven and to God.

What is the faith that thus has fought with and thus has conquered time? which comes to us as a dawning light from out the vale of Midian, from the solemn night of Passover, from across the desert, from the hoary mountain whose name stands consecrated to the latest age, from the devoted life and death of Moses, from the Psalmist's sweetest hymn, from the inspired page of prophecy, ever clearer and clearer, ever brighter and brighter, until perfect daylight shines upon the human soul?

Judaism proclaimed—and its voice yet sounds distinctly through the lapse of ages, whilst the deep echoes of the universe repeat it evermore—the unity of one almighty and eternal God, whose sovereign will is sole creator, whose infinite spirit fills all space and blesses all nature. It gave us a glimpse (all that man could bear) of the attributes of the Supreme Being that illumines with a moral glory His skies, His earth, His seas, and makes truth and holiness, love and mercy, the ministering spirits of His universe.

It revealed the great mystery of human life, it tells us that man is created in the image of God, of the beneficent, the merciful, the holy God; that we are endowed with a spiritual life, with qualities that are a reflection, a dim shadowing of some of the Almighty Father's attributes. It tells us, therefore, that mankind constitutes one universal family, all being alike the children of the one eternal God whose spirit dwells above, around, and within each human heart. It tells us that the affinity between God and man is an affinity of love, and that, in proportion as our minds are in unison with the divine mind, as we love and reverence more truly and deeply the pure, the good, and beautiful, as we consecrate ourselves more earnestly to holiness and truth, so the tie is drawn closer that unites us to the Divine Being.

Judaism, moreover, tells us that the solemn devotion of the heart and mind to virtue is at once the love and the worship of God; it is the offering to be laid upon the altars of eternal holiness, it is the song of praise and the voice of prayer.

Beautiful is the light that this revelation sheds upon the soul of man, upon the loving, desponding, beating, hoping, heart—upon the aspiring, thinking, toiling mind.   To those who realise the spirit of Judaism and accept its faith, earth and heaven, life and death, assume a new and glorious aspect.   Man's destiny, earth's discipline, life's purpose, and its closing scene, are made clear and bright.

The revelation that there is one God only, one almighty and eternal Father, holy, merciful, true, and pure, man's affinity to this Supreme Being, His divine love for man, gives us a faith, spiritual in its conceptions, great in its simplicity, and sublime in its clearness.   It explains at the same time the darkest enigma of human life ; and this enigma once solved, welcome are God's laws and ordinances, welcome the grief and joy, the trials and the warfare, the pain and the toil, for they are the teachers God sends to us to lead us to Him.   Welcome, too, the last great messenger, death, that comes to release the spirit from its worn-out tenement to bear it to immortality. Over the silent grave Judaism plants a glorious hope.   Even as dust to dust is consigned, it tells us that the liberated spirit returns to God, to carry on in a nobler sphere the great work commenced upon earth, to dwell more intimately and for ever in the light and the love of God. Even as Judaism proclaims that man is created in the image of God, so we build upon a sure foundation our hope of immortality. To the spiritual being that claims an affinity to the Eternal Mind there can be no annihilation or death. Betwixt a creature of dust and time, possessing only an ephemeral existence, and the Divine, the Infinite, and Everlasting, there could be no resemblance. The human mind must be so constituted as to progress onward and ever onward, developing in a future state the capabilities and power that have but their beginning here, or else we could not believe that we draw our spiritual life from eternal life. If man's moral affinity to his Creator be a truth, it follows that man's immortality is likewise a truth. Deriving its being from our being, a very part of ourselves, it needs no departure from the laws of nature, no resurrection of one man from the grave, no pale stiff corpse restored to life, for us to receive and believe this truth. The miracle, being a solitary exception, would weaken, rather than strengthen, our faith. Ours is an inner, not an outer evidence, the soul's hope and trust, the spiritual being's conviction, having its source in its own nature and in God's.

Such are the primal truths of Judaism, the simple elements of the faith that Moses proclaimed to the children of Israel, and that he committed to their care and love with his parting breath.

Such is the faith that imparts life to the pages of the Bible, that makes the Ancient Volume eternally young, fresh as a new creation from the hands of God.

It addresses itself not to time, or place, or varying circumstances, but to the human soul. It brings great and glad tidings to all men, tidings of things that have been from all eternity, for Judaism has its being in the nature of God and of man.

Were this not the case, time would long since have destroyed that which time had built; historical records may be lost or impaired, earth's monuments decay, creeds change, but that which is a living principle of nature, that which draws its existence from the mind itself, passes on from generation to generation, no matter beneath what sun those generations live and die.

Thus it is with Judaism; it existed in the eternal laws of the Divinity. The unity of God, His moral perfection, the love that illumines all nature, are truths that have their birth in eternity; and man's spiritual affinity to his Creator, the fraternity of the whole human race, these are truths that have existed since the first sigh and first hope made the human heart beat with sorrow or with joy. They were at different epochs conceived by a few great minds that outran their age, but were only fully revealed to the bondsmen of Egypt. Moses drew back the veil that concealed their glorious light. To him was given the blessed mission of imparting to his hapless brethren the faith that was to bless them and their descendants unto all ages, and to illumine the remotest end of earth by its moral and spiritual light.

Nobly did that mighty mind perform its ministry; calmly, clearly, beneath no cloud of mystic words, but with the simple majesty of truth and the eloquence of a deep conviction, was his great revelation proclaimed. It was given in the name and from God, and no thought or word of self mingled with the faith he announced to his brethren. It is a distinctive feature of Judaism, and perhaps an additional guarantee, if one is needed of its truth, that there is no man or hero worship in it; it exalts no human being into a divinity; it raises no altars but to the eternal, the one universal God and Father. Other faiths have their human embodiments of the Divine Being, they have their sculptured and their painted deities, they have intercessors between God and man, they have saints that perform miracles, and obtain blessings, and confer salvation. Their dead bones give life, their crumbling dust restores health, pilgrimages to their tombs propitiate the favour of Heaven. There is no monument of Moses save the Pentateuch; his burial-place remained unknown, lest it might lead to the worship of the man instead of God; and so in his life, his heroic, devoted, self-denying life, he guards his people against idolatry in every form. The worship of one only God, an invisible, spiritual Divinity, ever present, ever near, but never embodied, is taught by his great words and his great example. He paid himself to God this single truthful worship, and the world and himself were excluded from it. Judaism is therefore essentially intended to be a spiritual faith, and is consequently of all lands and times, to be more fully understood and realised, as the human mind attains a higher culture, a greater strength and purity.

Annexed to the moral law are ordinances of a ceremonial character, of a nature that appeals to the imagination, yet free from every taint of idolatry. They were an ignorant people to whom Judaism was revealed, and outward rites and ceremonies were an assistance to them, but they do not form part of the integral building, but compose merely its lighter and superficial ornaments, and many can be laid aside without injury to the main edifice.

Thus the temple, its sacrifices, its robed priests, and many of its rites, were for an early age and a young nation.

These have passed away, but in these the spirit of Judaism was not and is not bound up.

Its spiritual revelations and its moral law are alone permanent. These have their birth in the heavens above us, and in the soul of man; they fill the arched firmament with light and love, and satisfy the winged aspirations, the unutterable longings, and the quenchless hope of mankind.

With a Divine authority it gives forth its moral precepts, the eternal commandments, and these say to all men, to the old and young, to the great and lowly, to those that walk earth's sunny paths or tread its darkest track, where shadows hang deep and low, " You are the children of the Eternal Father."

" Thou shalt love the Lord thy God with all
thy heart, and with all thy soul, and with all thy
might."

" Thou shalt be holy, because I the Lord thy
God am holy."

" Thou shalt love thy neighbour as thyself."

These sublime precepts, unequalled in any faith
or creed, comprise practical Judaism.

The love of God, what does it not embrace?

It is the unsullied truthful worship, the heart
and mind's worship of one God, who is King,
Redeemer, and Father; it is the deep reverence
for holiness and virtue, which are the attributes
of the Divinity; it is the steadfast following the
path of duty, wherever that path may lead. It
is the vigilant striving after higher truth and
greater purity; it is the study of God's works, of
God's attributes, so that, by a fuller knowledge of
His moral perfection, we may better know and
better perform His Divine will.

The love of God is the holding our Almighty
Father, His holiness and His mercy, in a constant
remembrance, in the world, amidst its temptations,
its warfare, its revelry; in our homes, amidst our
families, by our children's cradles, by our loved
ones' graves.

The love of God is to hold Him in a remembrance that shall battle with sin and conquer

evil, that shall sanctify human affection, teach patience and resignation; a remembrance that, like a guardian angel, shall stand with outstretched wings between us and sin, between us and temptation, between us and despair — a silent watcher with smile serene over the green sod that covers earth's buried hopes and buried affections.

Such a solemn trust in God, such an earnest devotion to His will, such a faithful remembrance of Him, is what Judaism demands of us, when it says, "Thou shalt love the Lord thy God with all thy heart, and with all thy soul, and with all thy might." Sentiment and intellect, the heart's deepest feelings, the mind's noblest qualities, are to combine to render our offering of love acceptable to the Almighty Father.

This love is to be reared not in cloistral seclusion, nor in hermit's cell, but in the life God has appointed us. It is to be offered up not in synagogue nor house of prayer alone, but in the great temple built by God under His own blue skies, whilst nature's voice breathes forth her deep amen. It is to be an outward and a constant manifestation of the faith and light that dwells within the inner being.

"To love our neighbour as ourselves," the

second great precept, is to recognise that all men
are children of the Almighty God, are created in
His image, and have a holy claim to our sympathy and fellowship — monarch and beggar,
Jew and Gentile, all the great human family who
breathe, who think, who hope, who suffer, and
who rejoice beneath the wide heavens, beneath
the universal love of the Eternal Father.

It is to be an active principle, not a dormant
sentiment, but to give birth to merciful thoughts,
to generous deeds, to great and glorious labour
in the cause of humanity.   It is to act as a beneficent spirit, to conciliate, to reconcile, to for-
give, to link human hearts together in a holy
brotherhood so firmly and indissolubly that neither country nor creed, intolerance nor superstition, wealth nor poverty, can separate them more.

Judaism breathes forth this brotherhood; in all
her teachings it is almost her first and her last
lesson; we find it throughout the inspired volume, ever given in solemn words, even in the
name of God.

Our early history, the memory of bitter sorrows,
of Egypt's bondage, was to be kept alive, not as
a debt against, but a plea for mankind; as an in-
citement for us in all future ages to respect the
claims of a common humanity.   The recollection

of our own slavery was to teach us to confer freedom, the recollection of persecution was to awaken tolerance.

" Thou shalt not oppress a stranger: for ye know the heart of a stranger, seeing ye were strangers in the land of Egypt: the stranger that dwelleth with you shall be unto you as one born among you, thou shalt love him like thyself."

" Thou shalt not oppress a hired servant that is poor and needy, whether he be of thy brethren, or of strangers within thy land." " But thou shalt remember that thou *wast a bondman in Egypt,* and the Lord thy God redeemed thee thence: therefore I command thee to do this thing. When thou cuttest down thine harvest in thy field, thou shalt leave the sheaf in the field for the fatherless, for the widow, for the stranger. When thou beatest thine olive trees, thou shalt not go over the boughs again: it shall be for the stranger, for the fatherless, and for the widow. When thou gatherest the grapes of thy vineyard, thou shalt not glean it afterward: it shall be for the stranger, for the fatherless, and for the widow. And thou shalt remember that thou wast a bondman in Egypt."

It needed indeed, and needs still, a divine re-

velation to teach us that a true heroism consists
in forbearance and mercy, a true piety in tolerance and kindness; to teach us that grief, hardship, and persecution are to make us, the sufferers, stretch forth more freely the hand of
fellowship, to make us more and more merciful,
until, following the Divine example, we love and
compassionate all the human race.

These, then, are the two great practical precepts of Judaism, "the love of God, the love of
man." We may, and doubtless shall, as our
minds progress in the path of truth, give these
precepts a wider and a nobler interpretation than
we have hitherto done, and, above all, we shall
more faithfully fulfil them; we shall preach in a
higher and purer spirit, and practise what we
preach. But the spirit of Judaism will remain un-
altered, though we may understand it differently.
It comes from God to lead us to God. Like a
mighty river, it flows on and on, from land to
land and age to age, until it will finally lose
itself in the great sea of eternity. Let its moral law be but obeyed, its principles be carried
out in an enlightened manner, and how beautiful
a place our earth would be! What peace in our
homes, what truthfulness in the world, what love
and mercy everywhere! Then religion would be our

friend and guide, the link between man and man. In her name then kind words would be spoken, tears wiped away, and wrongs forgiven. In her name then there would be tolerance and freedom, a universal brotherhood. There would still be differences of creed, and rank, and opinion, and sect amongst earth's children, but all human beings would be linked together in the love of the Eternal God and the love of man.

Judaism has sometimes been called a religion of the past, and for those who content themselves with only its forms and its rites it may be a creed of gone-by times; but for those who realize its deep spiritual truths, who find that the Bible teaches us in part what God is and what we are, that its moral precepts train the mind to perfect itself from day to day, that its ceremonies are to be viewed as means, not ends, as symbols of, not the virtue itself,—to these it is a religion of the present and the future. If, unhappily, too many of us hitherto have held as sacred the letter instead of the spirit, if the love of ceremony has been dearer to us than obedience to divine precept, if holiness has been exercised more in the outer than in the inner life, if, in a mistaken zeal for the cause of Judaism, intolerance has usurped the place of brotherly love, it is time for us to awaken to a truer and a nobler conception of the glorious faith we hold.

This solemn festival is calculated to inspire thoughts that shall arouse us to a sense of its greatness. It leads us naturally to a consideration of what it has done for us and for mankind. In celebrating its advent we retrace its history; memory throws its light over the past, whereby we read all that it has effected for the human race. What great and noble things has it not revealed! what holy things has it not performed! Wherever its spirit has penetrated it has humanised the world, it has brought freedom to the enslaved, courage to the suffering, and hope to the weary. It has invested the human mind with a sanctity surpassing all worldly distinctions and honour. It has made life solemn and beautiful, giving it a glorious aim, and hope, and task.

And now its power is not diminished; as of old, it lifts up its solemn voice to lead us in the path of truth; as of old, it calls upon us to be the children of the Eternal God; as of old, it calls upon us to be holy, to be loving, to be merciful, to open our minds to all good influences, to all great truths, and reverently obey the Lord, the great revelations given us in the Bible, and the eternal law written in the human soul. "This commandment, which I command thee this day," says the Almighty God, "it is not hidden from thee, neither is it far off." "It is not in heaven, that thou shouldest say, Who shall go up to heaven, and bring it down, that we may hear and do it. But the word is very nigh unto thee, in thy mouth and in thy heart, that thou mayest do it."

Whenever we are true to the spiritual life within us, when we are true to our highest and noblest aspirations, then we are true to Judaism, for then and then only are we true to God.

There is no other faith by which mankind can be acceptable to the Almighty Father than the faith that makes us holy, true, merciful, and spiritually free. There is no other faith that can pilot our bark in safety to its eternal haven. The shores of time are strewed with wrecks, worldly pleasures, ambition, intolerance, bigotry, and idolatry; these are the false faiths, the ignorant pilots, that have shipwrecked so many.

Let us embrace Judaism, the divine, the pure, the beautiful, the faith of the Bible, the faith of holy minds and hearts, of the pure spiritual being.

Let us represent henceforth a true and pure

Judaism, realizing it in the sanctuary of our own hearts and homes, and in the face of the whole world. For this end we must acquire greater spirituality, greater truth, more liberal views, and nobler conceptions of our fathers' religion. For this end we must divest ourselves of old prejudices and superstitions, we must give freedom to the enslaved mind, letting it go forth free to learn and to unlearn, free to acquire knowledge and truth.

For this end we must diligently minister to the good of our brethren, solace the suffering, teach the ignorant, give courage to the weary, and impart by example, by love and mercy, that faith to others which is the mainspring of our own lives.

The task is great, but earth is the sphere of labour, and there is a glorious eternity for those who now abide and work in the hallowed faith that the Passover brought us in its glad deliverance, that the Bible proclaims in its pages, and whose voice, ever sounding stronger and stronger in the human heart, shall make itself universally heard and obeyed, until all nations and all people shall alike know and worship the only God, the eternal Lord and Father.

CHAPTER VI.

THE FEAST OF WEEKS.

IT was a beautiful ordinance of the Pentateuch that the first gathered fruits of summer should be consecrated to God, and that the harvest, earth's great festival, should be religiously solemnized.

It is a great epoch that brings us once again the chief sustenance of life, the common nourishment of all classes, the poor as well as the rich man's food. It is a great epoch that sends forth from every village and hamlet throngs of merry workers filling our fields and valleys with peaceful labour. It is a great epoch when in humble dwellings throughout the land there is the promise of bread for the coming winter—when toiling men and women may gather round their lowly hearth and caress their children with a smile upon their faces and a smile within their hearts. Life's dearest blessings, however, by their very frequence, sink into comparative insignificance. We almost require grief by the side of joy, shade by the side of light, to appreciate to their full importance the gifts of Providence.

Even when we recognise the good, we fail to trace it back to its source; even whilst we rejoice, the great Giver is forgotten.

As, year after year, the summer sun shines upon our fields, and the summer rain fertilizes them; as the green corn ripens till it waves its golden hair joyously in the noontide breeze, and harvest comes with its promise of plenty, with its hopes for winter frosts and snows, the gratitude awakened by the unutterable blessing is but feeble as compared with the good it secures. We welcome, indeed, an abundant harvest, for famine with its grim horrors, its wan face, its skeleton limbs, its fevered breath and desperate clamours, have taught us the value of a fruitful season. The agriculturist, the labourer, the merchant, and the poor man, watch with anxiety through long months the wind, the rain, the sunshine, and the mildew, for the prosperity of many, and the very existence of some, is bound up in the coming harvest. But when spring and summer have fulfilled their promise, when the rich ripe corn and the heavy barley are safely

garnered up and a wide-spread happiness smiles
upon the land, is there a universal and a deep religious sentiment awakened by God's great blessing?
Does the nation respond to the national good
secured by the Eternal Father's care; is the
prosperity, and joy, and wealth, consecrated to
God, who bestowed them? We do our moral and
spiritual nature a deep injury when we forget the
Almighty in His works and in His blessings.
When these are regarded as manifestations of the
Eternal Father's glorious attributes, then they lead
us to God by teaching us in part what God is,
and what we ought to be. We either grope about
Life's pathway as blind people, or we tread it
with enlightened minds open to receive divine influence and holy lessons from the beauty, the
love, the mercy, that are embodied and live in
the Almighty's works.

The Feast of Weeks was a solemn call to the
Jewish nation to worship God in His works.

During the consecration of the harvest all
labour was suspended in Judea. In the fields,
upon the hill sides, and in the city, a deep and
holy silence succeeded to the sound of human
toil. A day of rest and of devotion, a calm
Sabbath was solemnised in every Jewish home.

Rich and poor, strangers, the long separated,

but brothers in religion, assembled in the House
of Prayer, to offer up, as with one mind, to the
Eternal Father the thanks of a grateful people
and the love of grateful children.

Then, after this public and private dedication
of the harvest, when evening closed in and
families met in their homes, or on their terraces
in the cool starlight nights, there the summer's
first-fruits were eaten.

Thus celebrated, the harvest must have exerted
a deep influence upon the hearts of the people.
It awakened the sense, perhaps slumbering, of
God's paternal relation to man, and of His presence both in the outer and the inner life. It re-
minded all classes of their entire dependence
upon the Almighty, giving pride and conceit the
useful lesson that no human power can command
the first and common necessary of life, and bringing to the lowly the happy conviction that God
was with them in their daily labour, in their hard
and penurious existence. With a sense of his own
spiritual greatness and of the Almighty's Infinite love, must the labourer, side by side with
princes, have observed those solemn harvest feasts
in his Maker's house. The whole year of toil was
sanctified by this dedication of its fruits to God.

This pastoral life in Judea was a beautiful one,

calm and pure, simple yet dignified. It may well be one of the regrets of our present position that we are no longer an agricultural people. Whole generations live and toil and die in cities. The sweet influences, the holy teachings of the country, are almost unknown to the Jews. These have unhappily been exchanged for careworn and anxious vocations, pursued within city walls. The wealthy have seasons of leisure and freedom when they escape to brighter scenes; but our poor, when do they leave their dark streets and their narrow alleys? No mountain breeze or perfumed breath of rich meadow and pasture land, of trees and flowers, comes laden with health to our poor; no woods, with their pleasant coolness and their friendly shade, stretch their green arms around them. Of spring and summer's melody and beauty they know nothing; they only feel the lassitude of heat and the deep longing for fresher air, which increases as the grey stones they tread upon and the grey walls around them grow hotter and hotter beneath the lurid sun.

Earth's more favoured children, do you ever think of those little ones who pass all their infancy and youth in crowded courts and dark alleys? Do you think with a tender compassion of those who seldom or never see spring in her early verdure or summer in her gladness, who have never revelled in hayfields, never gathered wild roses and convolvuluses as they garland themselves along the green hedges; have never laid down wearied with sport amid violets and primroses, under spreading elms and waving beech, which form pleasant groves and long arcades in their sequestered forest homes. Shall these little ones never revel like yourselves in nature's sunshine amidst blithe freedom? Do you remember, as you visit the homes of our poor and working class which comprise the mass, how different a destiny was intended for the children of Israel? Do you remember that there is deep misery amongst us, though it is concealed from many, and the origin is forgotten, together with its effects?

A little wealth, a few personal enjoyments, the world's smiles—and the world has always smiles for the rich—cover up so prettily our errors and infidelities to God, that they are lost sight of. The surface wears a bright polish, and who would remove the superficial varnish to find out the dark spots and the imperfections that lie buried beneath? We are content to be as we are, except occasionally when truth will make itself seen and heard.

This day's festival, or rather this memorial of what once was a great and joyous epoch to a free and happy people, seems to tell us what we were and what we are. It places before us two distinct pictures. One represents the fertile valleys, the sunny banks of Jordan, the vine-clad hills of Judea studded with the dwellings of rich and poor : the other the dark streets, the close courts, the miserable alleys of densely-populated cities. The one shows us the agriculturist, the farmer, the tiller of the ground, the gardener, the labourer busy with cheerful activity, busy in bright valleys, fields, and groves ; the other shows us the slop-worker, the clothesman, the petty dealer, confined in their narrow dens or pacing the streets with a sad burden from early morning till late at night.

The one shows us a glorious temple, in which a united and free people pour forth from their hearts, song and psalm, and praise and worship, in purity and truth, the Eternal God and Father.

The other shows us synagogues beneath whose domes superstition and bigotry have usurped the place of religion ; where a creed enshrouded by misty traditions compiled in the dark ages, is taught instead of the pure and simple Judaism of the Bible; the faith that Moses bequeathed to his people.

The prophesies have indeed been realized. A blessing was promised upon our faithful adherence to the law—a law of holiness, of mercy, and of love—a curse was to follow its violation.

Its spirit was and is still violated, and the shadow of sin and of sorrow is upon us.

In vain the wealthy wrap themselves up in their worldly prosperity, in vain the bigoted clothe themselves in their Rabbinical holiness, in vain our priests pronounce their benedictions and their excommunications; the darkness and the blight of God's dispensation is upon us—and upon them.

Wander where we will, seek out new homes and foreign climes, go from city to city and synagogue to synagogue, still the shadow is there.

There ever remains the bright picture of the Far Past, whose colours time has not yet dimmed, and the sad picture of the present, with its gloomy tints and its miserable scenes.

And we do well to examine them both, to survey and track out, bring into the light of day, all the evils of our moral condition. They must be known and felt before they can be ameliorated.

We must probe the wound before we can heal it, we must investigate the disease before it can be alleviated.

There is much to do, but there is also much that can be done, and there never was a nobler field for human exertion. The violation of the law of God, the sublime and pure faith of our fathers, has produced the evils we deplore. The faithful adoption of Judaism, a true and spiritual Judaism, in our worship, in our homes, in our lives, and in our hearts, would restore the happiness and moral greatness of our people.

It is not God, but we, that have forgotten the covenant made with our fathers; it is not the Almighty who has ceased to be our Father, but it is we that do not give Him the love and reverence of children; it is not that the Bible contains no more a true and pure religion, but it is we that have forsaken her precepts and neglected her revelations to follow other doctrines and other teachers. It is not that the Spirit of the Eternal would not dwell as of old in the Jewish heart, making it the home of the pure, the beautiful, and divine; but it is we that have set up idols there, before which we bow down and worship.

Our first task is to return to Judaism, the Judaism Moses taught, that the Bible reveals, that the human soul, in its best and brighest moments, has conceived; the Judaism that demands of her disciples a spiritual worship, pure and holy lives, truth, mercy, and love.

This Judaism has to give a new life to our synagogues, it has to be preached from our pulpits, it has to purify our liturgy. It has to arouse our ministers to a nobler sense of their sacred duties, teaching them to profess and practise a religion that shall influence the inner more than the outward being. This Judaism has to be taught in our schools; it has to be made the ground-work of all education, the first lesson that the little child lisps upon its mother's knee, the first great thought that makes its heart beat with solemn hope.

This Judaism has to enter the arena of the world; it has to overcome superstition and intolerance, not by harsh weapons, but by words of peace and conciliation, by deeds of mercy and of love.

And this Judaism, whose ministry could be so great and beautiful amongst us, which could achieve such glorious things, is accessible to all. Her revelations are to be found where all alike may seek them—in the Bible, in the works of God, and in the human soul.

The sacred volume may have a place in every home, its words may shine upon every hearth. Above us are God's skies, around us are the wonders and glories of nature. In every human heart, the voice of conscience and of reason speaks. In these—in the hallowed book, in the great heart of nature, and in the soul of man— the spirit of Judaism dwells, and from out these she delivers her sacred oracles.

In the Bible we find the basis of our own and of all religions, the unity, the spirituality, the moral perfection of the Almighty, and man's affinity to his Creator, to his God, to his Father. We find clear and beautiful precepts, that enable man to carry on the work of moral progress. We find comfort, peace, and hope, a more permanent peace and a surer hope than the world can afford.

The Bible is the only work that does not grow old, and this stamps at once its divinity. A message from the Eternal Father to His children, its words are eternal. The theological writings of Rabbis or Fathers of the church bear upon their pages the dust and toil of time; and as the human mind progresses, it must necessarily shake it off and leave them behind.

They cannot therefore be permanent teachers, or legislators or lawgivers; we may revere their memory for the good they effected in their day, but we must pass onward to yet nobler and purer interpretations of the word of God; to yet more spiritual views of religion than they had conceived. Even as we occasionally visit, but do not dwell amongst the graves of the dead, so we may linger awhile among the relics of the past, but we must return to the living and the eternal.

Our young men, most especially those who are intended for ministers or teachers, should make the Bible their principal study. The Rabbinical writers of the early and middle ages may be read with profit if not considered as infallible or divine, for they throw a light upon the confused history, the sorrows, the persecutions, and the errors of our brethren. Here and there also, amid much that is the work of dark ages, of sophistry and folly, there are some beautiful things that shine from out the darkness, like stars that illumine a winter sky.

But for his daily food, for his guidance and his hope, let our youth look to the Bible.

Its sublime truths and broad precepts should be delivered from the pulpit. We do not want our ministers to quote and quote Rabbis without end, to repeat the commentaries of gone-by times, the precepts of fallible men like ourselves. We want them to preach, with the eloquence of truth, the Judaism of the Bible, a spiritual and living Judaism that knows no past. We want them to think for themselves, to speak from their minds to our minds, to sound the hearts of their brethren, and then pilot their way accordingly. We want to be instructed in the duties, not of the past, but of the present age, the great and noble age in which mankind has made so rapid an advance in civilization, in science, and in humanity. We want to think, and feel, and act with the living, not with the dead; we want to tread with manly footsteps the path of life, drawing ever nearer and nearer to virtue, to holiness, and to God.

Another source whence we gather a pure Judaism is from the works of God. We cannot love or realize the precepts of the Bible to ourselves, we cannot be good or great men, unless we love Nature—unless the beautiful, the calm—unless sunshine and storm—unless summer in her joy, and winter in his might, speak to us of God.

We must read the Eternal Father's glorious attributes upon His starried sky, upon the foam of ocean's waves, upon Alpine heights, upon fertile valleys, upon waving trees and fragrant flowers, or we cannot feel the beauty of the Psalms, or catch the inspiration of the Prophets. They turn to Nature to illustrate and portray the infinity, the spirituality, the love, the mercy of the Almighty God; and we must follow in their track and study Nature, or their words will never find their way to our hearts.

Quiet communings with Nature, in her secluded and peaceful haunts, would awaken purer thoughts and a truer and more spiritual devotion than years passed in investigating the old and time-stained volumes that fill our Rabbis and theologians' libraries. Let these be laid aside, and their readers go forth into God's own beautiful temple, into green fields, into woodland paths, into the calm country where the voice of happy Nature offers up its melodious praise to God, and they will acquire a love, a purity and truth, such as their old studies never brought them.

Let our infancy and our youth be taught to know and love God from out His works. There is no childhood so happy as that which is chiefly passed in the country, and a nobler and purer manhood succeeds to the blithe free days spent amidst Nature's sunshine and music.

And our poor—the little pale-faced city child— the toiling parent—the old and weary—who year

after year see the sun dawn from out fog and
mist, and set upon grey chimney stacks, or sink
behind grey walls without evening's mellowed
radiance—shall these be forgotten ?

They also must have their bright holidays,
their days of freedom to breathe God's pure air ;
to have His wide blue heaven above them, to see
and feel the beauty with which the universal
Father has surrounded His children.

If the wealthy would but give their poorer
brethren these days of enjoyment, how soon
would purer tastes and a deeper and truer religion grow up or be developed among them !
They would of themselves endeavour to follow
less degrading vocations, whilst nobler feelings
would lend a dignity to their labour, whatever
that labour might be.

It is a solemn duty for us to educate our poor
and working class, and every education where
the study of God's works does not form a part is
imperfect. Schools and synagogues alone will
not suffice to instil a pure Judaism; we must
enlist Nature as a teacher, or the work will be
marred, deficient in its most important feature—
its religious training.

There should be no school in which the pupils,
rich or poor, do not learn some of their noblest

lessons from Nature herself; there should be no community in which our working class are not enabled to enjoy a few free days amidst green fields, or by the sea-shore, or by the banks of cool rivers which reflect so brightly the smiles of summer.

Money thus spent would produce a greater good than we dream of; a good begun on earth to have its completion in heaven.

Our poor would return, it is true, to their city homes, to darkness and to noise, to toil and to fag; but they would bear back with them images of beauty with which they would tapestry their naked walls. They would bear back with them freer and more enlightened minds, truer conceptions of the Divinity; and from this new or this awakened sense of God's infinite love and mercy, of the beautiful and the holy, there would spring a happiness that gives both moral and physical health. The lowliest dwelling is beautiful when it is the sanctuary of a pure religion; the home of the poor man is holy ground when it is the home of truth, of love, and mercy.

Every one who has competence or wealth, or education or time, is bound to labour and provide for the intellectual and religious education of his poorer brethren. They have the highest claim to our sympathies and fellowship. They are, like ourselves, the children of the Eternal Father—they are created in God's image—they belong to the ancient race with whom God's covenant was made — they share our highest hopes, our deepest sorrows—they have to obtain the Almighty's forgiveness, living, even as we do, beneath the shadow of a heavy dispensation.

Upon this day, in which the children of Israel once celebrated so joyous a festival, the voice of the poor and the working class seems especially to plead to us, asking us not for alms, but for sympathy; for education, for the means of becoming an enlightened and religious people.

And to respond to their call we must give them a purer faith, a deeper reverence for the Bible, more spiritual teachers, and nobler interpretations of the word of God.

We must give them more air, more sunshine, more vigour. We must teach them to see and hear God in all things.

We must teach them to respect themselves as the noblest work of the creation, and to offer up to their God and Father the only worship that the Eternal accepts from His children—the worship of free minds, of pure and holy lives.

Be this our task, our work of love. A great

and arduous one; but there are already, to show us the way, devoted labourers amongst us, noble minds and true hearts, warm and strong with the love of man and the love of God.

There are some amongst us already who have professed and have endeavoured to practise and to teach a pure and true Judaism; let us follow in their footsteps, and unite with them bravely and boldly in their solemn and holy cause.

Then, as in the happy land where God's love was the light and the glory of His people, shall we consecrate our labour to God, a moral and spiritual labour, upon which we may pray for the Almighty's blessings, and to which we may humbly trust He will send a fruitful harvest.

CHAPTER VII.

THE JEWISH WOMAN.

" A noble woman, nobly planned
  To warn, to comfort, and command,
  And yet a spirit still and bright
  With something of an angel light."

THE Jews have been accused of following in the
wake of other Oriental nations, and of placing
woman in a comparatively low scale; we have
often heard it remarked that it was reserved for
Christianity to raise her to the same moral rank
as man—for the chivalry of the middle ages to
make her an object of tender devotion—and for
the civilization of modern times to remove her
from that flowery pedestal to a higher, though
perhaps less flattering sphere, where she is no
longer an idol to be worshipped by man, but his
fellow-worshipper, his fellow-labourer, and in all
things his faithful helpmate. Now we are not
going to dispute that the world has improved, or
to assert that the social position of woman has

M

remained uninfluenced by the progress of civilization, but we do not think that woman could
have been looked upon as an inferior being by
those to whom we owe the description of the
virtuous woman, in the last chapter of Proverbs.
We regard that beautiful picture as a refutation
of the assertion that the Jews made but small
account of female excellence; and we think that
the women of the present day could follow no
better model than that which was offered to the
women of Israel more than two thousand years
ago. Time may have hallowed it, but the mist
of ages through which it has descended to us
has not impaired its beauty or its usefulness.
Our poor sister in her dark home can follow that
bright example, and gain that which gold cannot
purchase; and the favoured ones of the world,
the inmates of luxurious dwellings, who without
toil or trouble enjoy a perpetual feast, must
strive to emulate it, or their prosperity will not
be happiness, their high station naught but care
and vanity.

Let us ponder for a few moments on that ideal
standard of female character, and try to discover
what are the qualities woman ought to possess
to approach, we will not say to attain it. Energy,
strength of purpose, and active zeal appear to us

among the most essential : they are not generally considered as such; perhaps, on the contrary, they sound to many ears unfeminine and harsh, but we contend that without them woman cannot even aspire to fulfil the task intrusted to her in the holy page; she may be gentle, nay more, kind at times, a pleasing ornament, approved of and smiled at by the world; but she will be far from the virtuous woman, she will not rejoice in time to come, nor will any rise up and call her blessed.

The virtuous woman " girdeth her loins with strength, and strengtheneth her arms," for she knows she must work hard to fill her appointed place in God's world. In a palace or in a cottage she must equally be a humble labourer in the service of her Master, and consider *that* her greatest honour here below. Her life is His gift, and she must not waste it in mere pleasure, in vain pursuits, nor in idle dreams, those baneful children of the imagination, which not only rob her of years of usefulness, but impair her mental powers and unfit her for all exertion.

" She looketh well to the ways of her household." She will feel herself bound, and it is no light or easy task, to make her home the abode of order, purity, and cheerfulness; daily to further the happiness of all in that small domain, and to maintain inflexible justice and impartiality among the little community who own her sway. Her children will be left to no foreign hands, she will guide and instruct them as far as she is able, and she will teach them by example, precept, and affection. She will not think she has fulfilled a mother's duty when she merely gives them the love and solicitude which are the natural instincts of her heart; she will look upon her children not only as her dearest treasures here, the joys of her youth and the consolations of old age, but as beings who greatly depend upon her for their happiness here and hereafter —beings she must prepare for this life and for eternity. All the powers of her mind and all the energies of her soul will be tasked to make her worthy of what she feels to be at once a blessed privilege and a fearful responsibility. For them she will, if needs be, give up pleasures and cherished pursuits; to their real welfare she will sacrifice a mother's vanity, and that blind fondness which is often but another name for selfishness or indolence; for them she will strive to improve her mental powers, to acquire knowledge, to learn patience, and practise self-control.

Then, when "her household are clothed in scarlet," that is to say, when all those dependent on her are cared and provided for, when her home is bright and peaceful, her children growing up in bodily and spiritual health under her vigilant eye, and her husband made happy by her care to satisfy his wishes and please his tastes, then let her not say, "My task is done;" another, and a blessed one, remains to be performed. "She stretcheth out her hand to the poor, yea, she reacheth forth her hand to the needy." Let her not deem it sufficient to open her purse, and distribute some of her superfluous wealth to the destitute, to appear as a subscriber in charitable lists, and to attend occasional meetings for charitable purposes—the power to give is one of the luxuries of the rich; in the exercise of it no self-sacrifice, no spirit of devotion is required, it is not "reaching forth her hand to the needy." Those simple words imply far more. There are the afflicted to console, the ignorant to instruct, as well as the needy to assist. To effect the former she must give not money, that genius of the rich, which appears at their call and does their work, but time, and trouble, and affectionate sympathy. She must not flinch from scenes of misery, nor from the prosaic, and to her perhaps revolting, details of real want; she must remember that those beings so poorly clad, so wretchedly housed, uncouth perhaps in manner, scorned, and, it may be, even degraded by misfortune and neglect, are children of the one great Father, sojourners here like herself, and, like herself, heirs to immortality. They have hearts like hers, which can be touched and softened by kindness, which will respond like hers to noble enthusiasm, and beat as tumultuously as her own for the dearly loved ones around her.

It is not mere pity that urges her to come to the aid of these weary toilers, who feed, clothe, and adorn her. A sense of justice and duty bids her rise from her luxurious repose, and stretch forth a gentle woman's hand, to heal their wounds, to raise them, if fallen, to console, refine, gladden them. She will impart to them what she has learnt herself from the good and wise, the living and the dead, and will thus return in some degree the debt she owes her poorer brethren; for does not their labour give her those precious hours of leisure which enable her to hold communion with the great teachers of the present and the past? Can she feel no gratitude for such a boon?

But she will often learn far more than she can teach; and many a time will she return from haunts of misery, humbled at her own inferiority to the patient, trusting, enduring sufferers she went to relieve.

"She openeth her mouth with wisdom, and in her tongue is the law of kindness." Wisdom without kindness wears a harsh, forbidding aspect, and kindness without wisdom would but too often prove no kindness at all. The virtuous woman combines the two; her wisdom is tempered and made graceful and winning by kindness; her kindness derives truth and power from wisdom—like the light and heat of the sun, they ought to be inseparable, and whilst the one enlightens, the other cheers with its genial warmth. Patient study and meditation must give her the former, humility and love the latter. They alone can repress the quick reply, the angry tone, and mocking word. And she must not forget that the law of kindness *extends to the absent*, and that it prohibits evil speaking and useless censure. Many are the temptations to break it, and hard must be her struggles if she would succeed in keeping within its bounds.

Vanity, frivolity, and indolence are perhaps the greatest opponents she will have to encounter;

let her combat them, then, with diligence and energy. And this confirms what we said some pages back, that the woman who would follow the model Holy Writ has placed before her must acquire strength of mind, power of application, and a pure and holy zeal, to urge her on to all that is good and great and noble. She must not only forbear and endure, but she must act, she must fulfil those manifold duties God has given her to perform. Active occupation will be the best antidote against the poison of vanity or the heartburning of discontent. Vexation, disappointment, and sorrow may doubtless still assail her; she may still have days of sadness and of gloom, when her heart is heavy with its secret load of grief; but she will not pine in discontent, she will not lead an aimless profitless life, mourning over what cannot be changed, wasting the present in vain regrets for the past, or in impossible reveries for the future. She will turn evil into good, by making it conduce to her moral improvement, and in alleviating the sorrows of others she will surely find consolation, perhaps even oblivion, for her own.

"Favour is deceitful; beauty is vain, but the woman that feareth the Lord, she shall be praised."

CHAPTER VIII.

ON IMMORTALITY.

THERE is one great hope that is shared by all mankind, more than a hope indeed,—a belief, a faith. The savage in his rude island home, amidst his barbarous companions and barbarous customs, the refined European amidst his pursuits of science and of art, the gray-haired sire about to close his long days, and the young child who has just begun to tread life's difficult path, all aspire to the same hope—the blessed hope of immortality.

Whatever may be our creed or country, our position and circumstance, we all feel that there is another world beyond the present one, invisible to human eyes, but one to which we are all bound. We all feel that death, mysterious death, that comes with cold hand to seal the lip, close the eye, and still the heart, has no power over the mind or spirit, but that it lives on eternally even whilst all things else die around us.

This faith being universal it would seem to be a natural instinct, and as such we might give it credence, for surely only a solemn truth, an inner and divine revelation, would have been implanted by the Creator in every human breast.

We have, however, an additional security for trusting to this hope, which man imbibes with his earliest breath, and which exhales from out the last faint breath he draws on earth.

To us the Bible comes to give the assurance that this life beyond death is no illusive dream or poet's fancy, but the greatest of realities— the first principle of human nature—the consummation of our earthly existence; and of all the Bible teachings this is at once the chief and the sublimest.

Where would be the interest of this life, so very brief and yet so sad, if it were not that we look upon it as a passage to eternity, and that we consider all its dispensations and trials, all its griefs and joys, sent to perfect the spirit for its final home? This intimate conviction sheds a glory and a beauty over human life, this exalts suffering and toiling humanity, this gives courage to endure, strength to resist, and hope to perform. This makes us look up to the Supreme Creator as our God, this makes us bend the knee in adoring

worship, and cry out in love, "Father! Father!"
for this conviction makes us know and feel that
we are not the creatures only, but the children,
the spiritual children, of the Infinite and Eternal,
of the Almighty Father.

We do well to furnish our memories and store
our minds with the evidences of immortality; for
the heart has its moments of despondency, when
its faith is shaken, and we seem, even as the inani-
mate things around us, made but to perish.

We do well to establish these convictions in
our minds upon the firmest foundation, whence
nothing may uproot them, for in all the wide
world we shall find none that will bring such
strength and solace, we shall find none that will
be so sure a guide and light, none that will lead
so effectually our thoughts and desires from
vanity and frailty to truth, and purity, and
God.

In all our households there is some vacant
chair, some missing step, some lost voice, some
empty cradle, that makes us yearn to believe
fully and trust firmly in that which, perhaps,
in earlier days, sufficed to us as an aspiration.
Mothers and fathers, who have wept bitter tears
over the green sod that covers your treasure;
husbands and wives, whose best happiness is now

the memory of departed things; stern manhood, whose ambitious hopes lie buried,—well may you open your Bible with a trembling eagerness to find in its time-honoured page a solace, aim, and hope, that lies beyond earthly vicissitudes and disappointments; and fortune's revellers and the treaders of sunshiny paths, they too may seek as anxiously even as mourners do, for the proofs of an immortality.

The grave, with its promise of everlasting rest, might, perhaps, be a prospect of comfort to the weary and care-worn, to those who, together with life, lay down a heavy burden, but to the prosperous and joyous the inviolable repose of the marble sepulchre and the darkness of the lonely vault would be appalling, but for the light and hope that shines beyond, but for the eternity whose glorious sphere gilds the horizon of this world.

Thanks be to God, to the Father of all mankind, who has given us a revelation of His merciful will and purpose—hath given us the hope that endows the lowly and the great, the sorrowing and the glad, the bereaved or the joyous parent of living children, with a calmness and an endurance, with a serenity and faith, that may lead them victoriously through all the changes of fortune, through all the trials, all the joys appointed them.

Young people, who would prepare yourselves nobly for your earthly destiny, for its pleasures and its sorrows, for its chequered scene, its sunshine and its shadows, open the ancient volume, and seek out the immutable hope held out to you there. Wait not to be weary, tempest-tossed, or shipwrecked, before you inquire of the safe harbour, before you learn to steer your bark to the shores of eternity. Come now and peruse the treasures of ages, that, thank God, lie within the reach of us all.

In the Book of Genesis, the first book of the Bible, we find an announcement of immortality, in the words that proclaimed that " man is created in the image of God." We know that our frail and decaying bodies could not have been created in the likeness of the Eternal God, that the impress of Divinity could not be stamped upon crumbling dust and mouldering clay, therefore we must be endowed with a spiritual nature, whose attributes shall in some measure be like the attributes of the Supreme Being, and which shall outlive decay and time.

Moses, the inspired servant of the Almighty, confirms this glad tidings to us in his supplica-

tions for himself and his brethren.   He addresses
God as the "Lord, the God of the spirits of all
flesh," thus telling us and all mankind that we
possess a mind and an inner life distinct from
the corporeal frame, and that this spirit can
alone worship God.

The whole of the Pentateuch, its spiritual revelations, and its moral precepts, are significant
of immortality, for the religion that proclaims
our affinity to the Supreme Being, that teaches
us to be holy, pure, and true, because God is all
holiness, truth, and purity, would belie itself,
if it were only addressed to creatures of dust;
for, were this world all, our faculties would be
extinguished before they had time to put forth
their full development.   The bud and blossom
would be destroyed before the fruit could ripen.
There is nothing in nature that does not seem to
carry out the purport of its creation, and shall
man, with his unfathomable thoughts, his aspiring
hopes, with his love of the great, and beautiful,
and good, with his yearning after a holier, nobler
life than the present one, shall his existence alone
be incomplete and unfinished ? Shall it cease before his task is done, before those thoughts are
answered, those hopes realized, before he has
seen his ideal visions of truth and virtue em-

bodied? Even as the hallowed book calls forth these aspirations and these images, so does it also give us the assurance we need, that they are not given fruitlessly for a brief and transient day, but given to be perfected and carried out in eternity.

In the Psalms we find abundant proofs of David's deep conviction of immortality; and how many tempest-tossed minds and sorrowing hearts has the Psalmist's deep trust in eternity sustained and strengthened!

He says, in his heart-thrilling prayers to his God and Father, "Thou wilt not leave my soul in hell; neither wilt thou suffer thy Holy One to see corruption." "Thou wilt show me the path of life: in thy presence is fulness of joy; at thy right hand there are pleasures for evermore."

And again, in a time of tribulation, he says, after supplicating God, "The Lord redeemeth the soul of his servants; none that trust in him shall be desolate." "How excellent is thy loving-kindness, oh, God; therefore the children of men put their trust under the shadow of thy wings." "They shall be abundantly satisfied with the fatness of thy house, and thou shalt make them drink of the river of thy pleasures. For with *thee is the fountain of life, in thy light shall we see light.*"

The 49th Psalm is a glorious witness of the sublime hope that man clings to when this world gives way beneath him. If memory cannot give it pure and fresh from out her repositaries, turn to it now; there are few of us whose thoughts have not required the solution given there—few of us that have not been troubled at the inequality of our lot, at the apparent glory of the bad rich man, the sorrow of the poor but good man. In this psalm we find the answer to our questionings and our disquietude, and our envy ceases as the vision of better and eternal things is presented to our minds.

In the life of David we find a touching incident, that shows us that his faith in immortality was a faith of the heart and mind, not displayed in psalm and prayer only, but in his own actions, exercising a mighty influence over all his thoughts and feelings. When his well-loved child was struggling with a mortal illness, David lay in ashes upon the bare earth, weeping and fasting. The child died, and his servants were afraid to tell him of its death, lest his grief, so great before, whilst yet he had hope, should be excessive now—that hope was gone; but when their sad faces and whispers informed him of it, he rose from the ground, changed his apparel, went into the house of God, worshipped at the altar, and on his return home eat the bread prepared for him. " What is this?" inquired the servants; " Thou didst fast, and weep for the child whilst it was alive, but when the child was dead, thou didst rise and eat bread;" and David said to them, "Whilst the child was yet alive, I fasted and wept; for I said, Who can tell whether the Lord will be gracious to me, that the child may live; but now he is dead, wherefore should I fast? can I bring him back again? I shall go to him, but he shall not return to me."

Memorable words! O fathers and mothers who have wept and prayed by your children's side, and seen inexorable death come, in spite of all your tears and watchings, take comfort at these words. The loved ones are gone indeed, never more shall they gladden you on earth, never more shall their bright faces and joyous voices fill your homes with happiness, never more shall they return to their familiar places, but you, *you* shall go to them—you shall meet again, love again, rejoice again in the home of eternity.

In the Book of Ecclesiastes, in the Preacher's parting words, we have a solemn testimony to immortality. They were written when age had taught him a life-long experience, when, after having enjoyed all possible prosperity, he proclaimed that all of earth is vanity. He describes touchingly our closing days, when the world's pleasures and glories fade away, and the shadows of night draw round us, and he says, " Then shall the dust return to the earth as it was, and the spirit shall return to God who gave it."

In the page of prophecy the subject of our future existence becomes more frequent, and a clearer light is thrown upon it. Isaiah, in his sublime inspirations, speaks thus of the great hereafter, and we feel that he speaks with the Spirit of the Almighty upon him :—

" God will destroy in this mountain the face of the covering cast over all people, and the vail that is spread over all nations. He will swallow up death in victory, and the Lord God will wipe away tears from all faces."

And further on, in addressing the house of Israel, he says, " Thy dead men shall live, together with my dead body shall they rise. Awake and sing, ye that dwell in the dust; for thy dew

is as the dew of herbs, and the earth shall cast
out the dead."

We have in a vision of Ezekiel's a vivid picture of the day when the earth shall give up her
dead. We must cite it all, as it is an answer to
the many doubts, and sophisms, and misgivings
that may rise up in our minds, upon the truth
of which faith in God alone can give us the
assurance.

"The hand of the Lord was upon me, and
carried me out in the spirit of the Lord, and set
me down in the midst of the valley which was
full of bones, and caused me to pass by them
round about: and, behold, there were very many;
and, lo, they were very dry. And he said unto
me, Son of man, can these bones live? And I
answered, O Lord God, thou knowest.

"Again he said unto me, Prophesy upon these
bones, and say unto them, O ye dry bones, hear
the word of the Lord. Thus saith the Lord God
unto these bones; Behold, I will cause breath to
enter into you, and ye shall live: and I will lay
sinews upon you, and will bring up flesh upon
you, and cover you with skin, and put breath in
you, and ye shall live; and ye shall know that I
am the Lord.

N 2

"So I prophesied as I was commanded: and as I prophesied, there was a noise, and behold a shaking, and the bones came together, bone to his bone. And when I beheld, lo, the sinews and the flesh came up upon them, and the skin covered them above: but there was no breath in them. Then said he unto me, Prophesy unto the wind, and say to the wind, Thus saith the Lord God; Come from the four winds, O breath, and breathe upon these slain, that they may live. So I prophesied as he commanded me, and the breath came into them, and they lived, and stood upon their feet, an exceeding great army. Then he said unto me, Son of man, these bones are the whole house of Israel: behold, they say, Our bones are dried, and our hope is lost. Therefore prophesy and say unto them, Thus saith the Lord God; Behold, O my people, I will open your graves, and cause you to come out of your graves, and bring you into the land of Israel. And ye shall know that I am the Lord, when I have opened your graves, O my people, and brought you up out of your graves, and shall put my spirit in you, and ye shall live."

We are told plainly in this prophecy that death cannot annihilate or have dominion over us; but that God's Spirit will breathe upon us, even after the grave has covered us and we are crumbling dust, a life eternal.

Daniel, the wise and beloved servant of God, tried and found faithful, both in adversity and prosperity, bears witness to the same truth, and in words that should be engraven in indelible characters upon our hearts :—"And many of them," he says, "that sleep in the dust of the earth shall awake, some to everlasting life, and some to everlasting shame and contempt. And they that be wise shall shine as the brightness of the firmament, and they that turn many to righteousness as the stars for ever and ever."

We cannot conclude our citations from the Bible with a more glorious attestation of immortality than these words; but there are many more scattered through the sacred volume, and it is a task we should all perform to trace them out and chronicle them in our minds.

Now that we have seen how true and sure is this promise of eternal life, it behoves us to inquire what effect it produces upon us; whether it influences our daily life, or whether it abides as a silent hope within us, whose voice is only heard upon a few eventful epochs.

That all mankind will participate in a life

hereafter is a pledge of the Almighty God, is a covenant of the Bible, is a law of human nature; but whether it will be one of happiness or of misery, of glory or of shame, must depend upon ourselves. Our life on earth must decide our future destiny. Not our poverty or our wealth, not our talent or our ignorance, not our noble or our lowly name, not our outward forms or rites in worship, but the thoughts and the feelings, the hopes and the faith that God alone, not man, can see and judge.

Everlasting glory or shame, according as we have loved our God in truth and purity, as we have striven to obey His will, the will that is revealed to us through our conscience, through our reason, and through the Bible.

Glory or shame eternal, according as we have borne our burden patiently or our prosperities meekly, according as we have struggled with sin, battled with temptation, as we have loved our brethren with a holy love, as we have helped them, taught them, forgiven them, as no intolerance, prejudice, or passion has made us forget that *our* God is the God and Father of all mankind, that every human soul bears the Divine image upon it, and is, like ourselves, immortal.

Glory or shame, as we have sought to perfect ourselves, to cultivate our minds, to purify our hearts, as we have remembered through all earth's changing scenes the life eternal.

Most solemn, most glorious of all truths is this, that we in our earthly life frame our future one—that we plant here the seed that is to bear fruit in eternity—that here we commence what shall have no end. Let us endeavour to realize this truth, and so live and so act that it bear not witness against us hereafter. Knowing that this is but a brief existence, let us not cling to things of earth, to idols of clay, to the vanities and follies that float adown the stream of time, but that are lost before they reach the sea of eternity. Let us consecrate ourselves, our minds and hearts, our fortune and our time, our love and our worship, to the good and immutable, to the true and divine, to that which shall outlive time, and stand with us in the presence of God, in the home eternal.

House of Israel, dispersed and outcast race, so fallen from your high estate, to you, to whom earth brings but little honour or fame, this blessed hope of immortality most especially addresses itself. Take hold of it, grasp it in such wise that it shall be a reality, a faith to you, ever present, ever living within the sanctuary of your heart, so that through all your dispensations and your sorrows, through your thorny path and clouded way, through prejudice and contempt, or through fortune and luxuries, through all the vicissitudes of human fate, from eager hoping childhood to weary trembling age, you may be led calmly and truthfully, serenely and cheerfully, to virtue, to purity, to God, to everlasting peace and glory.

CHAPTER IX.

THE ISLAND OF JEWELS.

IT was a fine summer's day—an English summer's day, not oppressively hot—when it is a delight to breathe the warm pleasant air, doubly pleasant if it comes loaded with the fragrance of new-mown hay, or the perfume of some neighbouring hawthorn blossom, as it came to me through my open cottage window. "Well," said I, in answer to the inviting breeze, "I will go out, and leave off pondering on that dark entangled web, human life; and, with beautiful joyous nature around me, forget man's troubled existence." I raised my head from its drooping position, closed my books, locked my desk, and sallied out. But, like my own shadow, thoughts of sadness followed me into the bright sunshine of my garden, and I could not escape from the latter any more than from the former. The birds warbled in vain to me, the flowers I loved so well sent me consoling words in their language of sweet

odours : but they spoke in vain. Man's destiny
appeared to me only the more wretched by com-
parison with the fairy scene in which he performs
his little part.   And yet no great misfortune had
befallen me—death had not thrown his withering
shadow upon my home—no ardent hope had
been suddenly blighted—but I was suffering
from a load of little cares and disappointments;
efforts strenuously made for what I thought
laudable objects had been unsuccessful; long-
cherished plans had come to nought; I had seen,
that morning too, poverty which I could not
relieve, heartburning for which I could find no
balm.   Every one seemed to me perhaps a reflection of myself, unfit for the situation he was
placed in, wearing out his little span of life in
discontented murmurings, and among this miserable crew I felt myself a most miserable, useless
being.

Having walked three times round my garden,
without coming to any more agreeable conclu-
sion, I opened the wicker gate, and, brushing
ruthlessly through the clematis which overarches
it, strewing the path with a shower of its snowy
flowers, I walked rapidly away from the garden—
away from the shady lanes I liked best to saunter
in—away from the village—and, above all, away

from the infant school, for the sound of children's careless laughter would have caused my tears to flow. I walked on towards the sea, but many old friends were sunning themselves on the beach, and I felt sure that William would torment me to take a sail—old Jim would insist upon my looking through his telescope at that white speck yonder—and Tom, my devoted naturalist, would fill my hands with curious weeds, just torn from their rocky homes to grace my herbarium—and I fled from all those intrusions upon my solitude by a narrow zigzag path up to a lonely part of the downs, which, from its uninviting aspect, I had never visited before.

Throwing myself down there upon the short warm grass, I gazed upon the wide expanse of ocean—upon the broken cliffs, with their sharp cutting shadows and brilliant lights—and, unlike the flowers and the birds, the little waves murmured in a plaintive voice of sadness, care, and death. Their influence was soothing, and looking into that ocean was like looking into the glistening eye of some dear friend—out of its mysterious depths came sympathy and comfort. And as I gazed in a more tranquil mood, I became fascinated, as it were, by one pale green strip of water, which looked like a floating ribbon gently waving in the blue sea. And the ribbon became larger and less transparent, until it seemed no longer of the same element as the surrounding water. The longer I looked at it the more it seemed to increase in size and density; its surface was broken into various forms, marked by lights and shadows; colour became mixed with varied tints—now hills and woods appeared upon it, and long rivulets wound their silver threads through the wondrous scene. But as it grew into a large island a mist arose upon the sea, and formed a band around it, which concealed its margin, but left the interior clear and distinct; indeed, the sun's rays seemed to centre there, and the atmosphere, pure and transparent as that of a southern clime, allowed me to see its smallest details.

And now emerged from the mist on the eastern side of the island moving living forms. I half expected some strange sea-nymphs and mermaids, and was somewhat disappointed on finding only the likenesses of my old well-known brother and sister, man and woman. I soon became, however, interested in them, and anxious to learn whence they came and whither they were bound; for they all moved in one direction—from east to west. Some appeared to enjoy their journey, and rather danced than walked along; others, on the contrary, looked weary, as if the way was long and tiring; and a few seemed so weak and tottering that it was painful for them to proceed, but yet they moved on at the same pace as the strong and the hearty. Many cast wistful glances back to the east, but none ever returned, none even ever paused or rested for one moment; and I thought I heard a rustling wind behind the travellers urging them on. All proceeded in the same direction, but by different paths; some were toiling up steep hills, others moving pleasantly in flowery meadows; one traveller entered the deep gloom of a forest, while another walked through a sunny garden. But the east wind blew upon them all alike, and murmured "On, on;" and the hills were ascended, and the dark forests crossed, and, alas! the meadows and gardens also, and other paths, some rugged and some pleasant, were trodden by these restless islanders.

Differing from each other in almost every respect, these fellow-travellers had one point of resemblance, which seemed to indicate they had some common mission to perform—each carried in his hand a small casket of rock crystal, at the bottom of which a few lines were engraven.

I remarked that on the eastern side the caskets seemed nearly spotless, but that as their owners advanced they became soiled, and many even were much defaced with stains; but I perceived also that some became enriched with precious stones—these arranged themselves into letters, and formed words. On one casket—its owner had just emerged from an ugly ravine—I read in ruby letters, "Faith;" on another, written in deepest sapphire, "Charity." And when the casket was adorned with many of these brilliant words it shone so brightly that it shed a beautiful lustre around.

"Is it to beautify these precious caskets that these beings are journeying here?" thought I. "Ah, no, that cannot be; for many never look at the gem they almost unconsciously carry, and of the stains that spoil its purity, only busy themselves with gathering the blossoms they find on their way. There is one fair young traveller decking herself with garlands of flowers, heedless of the stains the rose-leaf and the violet make upon her casket; there is another picking luscious fruit, and the juice falls upon his casket and leaves a blemish. And there is another, and, I suppose, a wiser traveller, for he smiles with contempt at those two careless beings, and

even tells them that all they have amassed is
frail, perishable, and profitless. And his arms
were filled with gold and silver, and on his back
he carried a load of precious sweet-scented wood,
and I admired his industry, his patience, and his
self-denial, which enabled him to leave untouched
the beautiful flowers and tempting fruit he
passed by, and to toil on for the lasting gold.
" Doubtless," thought I, " these travellers are
obeying the orders of some king, and bringing
him the treasures of the island. The flowers,
the fruit, and the gold are to be taken to some
distant shore, but the former will certainly
wither and decay before they reach their new
home; truly wise is the man who carries the
latter load—his burden is heavy, but his treasure
is lasting, and his toil will not have been vain."
And as this man advanced towards the western
limit a sunbeam burst through the mist, and,
resting on the shore of the island, looked to me
like a golden bridge uniting this with some
unseen land. Then, to my astonishment and
grief, I saw the load of palm and cedar branches
fall from his back, the gold and silver escaped
from his trembling grasp, and the waves seemed
to roll them into the interior of the island again.
Bereft of all he had so anxiously amassed, the

poor man stepped upon the sunbeam with the unheeded casket in his hand, and, shrouded in the closing mist, his form was soon lost to me.

Perplexed and dissatisfied at what I had seen, I bewailed the hard fate of these poor travellers, who laboured for nought, and who seemed so ignorant during their journey of what must happen at its termination, and my interest increased by pity. I watched three new-comers in the island with curious attention. One I heard called Learsi, the second Felicia, and the third Yresim. When I first saw them they were all three walking in a beautiful garden quite at the eastern side of the island; they all looked blithe and joyous, and in that lovely spot they could hardly have been otherwise. The trees seemed only just to have burst into leaf, of so fresh and tender a green was their foliage; and the plants, which had been sown by no niggard hand, were covered with opening buds, rather than full-blown flowers. But what I thought more beautiful even than the blushing buds and the light young leaves, were the travellers' caskets—their crystal was nearly spotless; they were so admirable in their purity that I was never tired of gazing at them. And happiness beamed upon the travellers' faces, and they talked to each other of the beauty of the garden, and of the kindness of the monarch who had sent them to such a pleasant abode. But I felt only intense compassion for these poor ignorant beings; for I saw that the garden was not large, and beyond it were waste lands and barren moors.

Yresim was the first to leave the garden: the flowers became scarcer upon his path, the trees few and dwarfed, until they disappeared, and Yresim found himself upon the unsheltered moor. Surprised and sorrowful, Yresim turned a tearful eye to the pleasant scene he had quitted, and where his former companions were still revelling among sweet-scented bowers; but soon he brushed away the unmanly tear, and reading the words engraved on his casket, which seemed to act as a talisman upon his spirits, walked unrepiningly on. As he proceeded the climate appeared to change, a cold wind swept over the desolate moor, and Yresim folded his cloak around him, but it had been torn by some brambles on the road, and it did not seem to shield him from that chilling blast; he shivered with cold, and his face looked pale and pinched. The path became, too, more and more rugged. Yresim's feet were often cut by sharp stones, and he limped as if in pain.

At last, overcome by cold and suffering, the
lonely traveller seemed to me to be measuring
with his eye the distance that separated him
from the western limit of the island, and he
sighed repeatedly when he saw how long it still
was; and then he turned to his casket, but its
crystal was dimmed by those heavy sighs, and
he tried now in vain to decipher the words which
were written in it. And then an expression of
anguish came over him, and he looked to the
right and to the left at the more fortunate travellers, whose paths, unlike his, were pleasant and
cheerful, with a look of envy, almost of hate.
"Ah, why can I not follow them?" he murmured; "why are they allowed to bask in the
sunshine, and I forced to strive against this
biting wind? Where is thy justice, great King?
where thy mercy?"

Yresim now found himself at the foot of a
steep hill, and my heart bled for the poor weary
traveller, with such a barrier to cross, and not
even the pleasant words in his casket to cheer
him on his way.

He began the ascent with trembling limbs and
downcast eyes, and his pallor seemed to increase
with every step, and his cloak to become more
tattered and useless. Suddenly a rustling sound

attracted his attention, and, looking up, he saw
at a little distance from him, but in the same
rugged difficult path which he was so painfully
treading, a fellow-traveller. The latter bore the
same signs as Yresim of cold, want, and fatigue;
but yet, strangely enough, I thought he did not
look unhappy. He was diligently employed
picking up stones. These I soon perceived to
be precious gems, which arranged themselves
into glittering words upon his casket, and I read
on it " Resignation" and " Fortitude." And
these words reflected such a beautiful light upon
the traveller's thin pale face, that I felt more ad-
miration than compassion for him.

His example was not lost upon poor Yresim,
and he, too, began searching for these blessed
stones, for some time, however, without success.
Having observed that the traveller repeatedly
consulted the words in his casket, he turned to
his, and wiped away the moisture from the
crystal, which became clear and transparent
again. Yresim then read with avidity the words
which had so long been hidden from him, and
as he read and pondered on their meaning I
thought his face became more hopeful, and soon
I saw some precious stones glittering in his
hands, and he placed them on his casket, and I

read there in emerald letters, " Trust," " Faith," and " Courage."

The hill was still high and steep, but Yresim murmured no more, and in the most rugged spots he generally found some gem or other, so that by the time he had reached the summit his casket was richly adorned. And now he has gained the platform, and he looks back on the way he had toiled up with an expression of satisfaction, nay, almost of pleasure; then, turning to the radiant west, repeats a short but fervent thanksgiving.

The descent was easy—though here and there were brambles—and, on the whole, the path was smooth and pleasant; but Yresim was now near the end of his journey, and the island, with its pleasant spots and dreary wastes, must soon be left for ever.

I perceived that the western shore was very different from the eastern. Here there were no beautiful gardens, with variegated flowers glowing in the sunshine, but quiet shady groves instead; and through the branches of the dark trees Yresim gazed into the deep blue heavens. And now he is so near the shore that he hears the waves beating against it, and feels the ocean's damp breath upon his brow, and his casket shines

brighter than ever, as, with it clasped in his up-
lifted hands, he mounts the golden arch, and—
but I strained my eyes in vain, I could follow
him no more.

I then tried to discover his two early companions. They had both left the garden where
I had first seen them. Learsi was walking in a
deep valley, which led to a dark forest; and
Felicia was crossing a sunny meadow, fragrant
with flowers from every clime. Here the blue-
bell and primrose grew under the shade of the
pomegranate, the white flowers of the myrtle
received a slight blush from the scarlet poppy
beside them, and the wood anemone and celan-
dine mingled their fresh field perfume with the
richer odour of tropical plants.

Felicia looked bright and happy as when I
last had seen her; robes of the softest material
hung in ample folds round her graceful form,
and her waving hair, on which sunbeams seemed
to be ever gleaming, formed a fitting frame of
gold for her fair dimpled face, the very type of
joyous beauty.

The absent are often brought as vividly to
mind by contrast as by resemblance; and when
I saw this beautiful being gliding along the
flowery meadow, the pale attenuated form of

Yresim appeared before me, wrapping his tattered cloak about his shivering limbs, and almost involuntarily I repeated his cry of despair—" O King, where is thy justice?"

Felicia, in the meantime, was adorning herself with flowers, rainbow garlands were twined around her white garments, and a wreath of dark violets enhanced the brightness of her hair, and before these had time to fade she had culled fresh ones from that paradise of flowers. As I continued watching her, however, I thought I could discover symptoms of weariness, or rather discontent; she would sometimes throw away her fairest wreaths — trampling them under foot, and would eagerly choose other flowers, of rarer growth, perhaps, or richer scent, but these likewise were soon exchanged for new ones, which seemed, in their turn, to please but for a very short time. But at last, although she continued to gather and arrange the flowers which grew so profusely around her, all pleasure and zeal in the occupation appeared gone, listlessly she picked those fragrant blossoms, and listlessly scattered them again.

She now entered a grove of orange trees, and as she walked through that golden shade I thought a degree of joyousness seemed to return

to her. The rich clustering fruit, the mossy
carpet she was treading on, and the canopy of
green branches, upon which birds of wonderful
plumage, and insects which must have been
winged gems, were darting about like meteors
in a northern sky, formed a novel scene which
appeared to interest and please her; the long
absent smile parted her lips again, and her eyes
shone with something of their former lustre.
But why does she start and turn pale, and bend
her head forward, as though she were listening
to some ill-boding sound? I can only hear the
murmur of rippling water. But as that sound
grows louder, her alarm seems also to increase;
she looks back, and tries to retrace her steps,
but the pitiless east wind whispers hoarsely "on-
wards," and with blanched face and trembling
limbs she proceeds. But as she walks on, the
oranges wither, and dead leaves fall noiselessly
but sadly to the ground. In a few moments she
has passed the now mournful grove, but she has
not entered the bright sunshine again; heavy
clouds darken the sky, and a thick mist has
arisen, veiling the landscape within its impal-
pable curtain.

Felicia looked neither at the clouds nor at the
mist, for there, at a few yards before her, was

the cold dark wave, and each unwilling tottering step she took brought her nearer to it. The poor faded flowers fell one by one from the form they had adorned, and under garlands and wreaths appeared Felicia's till then unheeded casket; for the first time she now examined it, but the stains of flowers rendered it almost impossible to decipher any of the words engraven in it. Alas! alas! where can she look to for consolation, for help? above are the angry heavens—behind, the scenes she may not return to —before her the fatal water, reflecting the dark clouds, and bounded by the mysterious mist. Tears, hot scalding tears, fell from that disconsolate one; and I heard, though indistinctly, from her pale quivering lips, words of sorrow, fear, and remorse. And now her feet touched the dreaded brink, and soon the silent wave encircled her, and a fearful struggle ensued between that fragile being and the ever-deepening waters. Every moment she sank deeper and deeper, and at last I could only perceive a white speck upon the dull gray water.

But the mist gradually cleared away, and I discovered at no great distance the opposite bank: thus, it was not the great boundless ocean, after all, but only one of the rivers of the island;

and Felicia, the same, yet how unlike, appeared mounting with difficulty the slippery bank. The work of years seemed to be accomplished in that short space of time, for youth, mirth, and beauty had departed from her. Felicia's eyes were bent upon her casket, which had regained much of its original purity—the water of the river, or her tears, perhaps, had washed off many of its stains, but it was adorned with no precious stones, and as the traveller gazed sorrowfully at it, she whispered faintly, " Not one single jewel have I found during my long pilgrimage." But at that moment something shone upon the bank, like fallen tears among the weeds; Felicia stooped, however, took up the sparkling drops, and placed them on her casket, where they formed the word " Humility."

Whilst thus employed she met Learsi, her old companion in the spring garden. Toil and grief had left their ineffaceable marks upon him, but there was beauty still in the pale lofty brow, all furrowed as it was, and in the bright unquenched fire of his eye. An exquisite light shone upon his face, and seemed to throw a halo of glory and purity around him. This beautiful light emanated from his casket, which was covered with jewels; among them, but larger and brighter than any, shining like stars taken from heaven's own mine, appeared the words "Charity" and "Brotherly Love."

Felicia seemed attracted by their dazzling beauty, and begged Learsi to tell her how and where he had found such matchless gems. "Matchless they are by no means," replied Learsi, "there are many larger and finer in the island; and if you search for them, following the written directions of our King, you will doubtless find them. But, tell me, where have you been since we parted, and what have you acquired to take back to the Monarch who has sent us?" Felicia hung her head as she pointed to her poorly-adorned casket, and then related to him the scenes that I had witnessed.

"Yes, yes," exclaimed Learsi, when she had finished, "we are strangely blind, and our eyes must be rudely opened by the cold blast on the moor, by the fearful waters of the river, or by the sharp fingers of thorns and brambles, or we see not the jewels around us."

"What becomes then," said Felicia, "of those whose path is ever among flowers?"

"Where is that path?" replied Learsi; "no

traveller in the jewelled isle ever has found it yet, methinks."

"Ay," returned Felicia, with a sigh, "we are sent indeed upon a hard dismal journey."

"Hard and dismal truly we might call it, notwithstanding its beautiful eastern garden, its many sweet-scented glades, and its glorious views, were not priceless jewels the reward of our toil and pain. Do not let us malign this island where are found the talismans without which the gates of our distant radiant home will never open to us."

"But you have not told me where you found those precious gems," said Felicia, "and I am all impatience to learn."

"I had wandered through many varied scenes," began Learsi, "when I found myself in the middle of a large gloomy forest; my thoughts were as dark as the atmosphere around me, which received no light from the sun, but was only fitfully illumined by the fire-fly and glow-worm. Whilst I was thinking how sad and dismal was my path, I heard half-stifled sobs of some poor travellers, who seemed still more affected than I was by that strange darkness. And I felt intense pity for my fellow-pilgrims, and tried with all my might to clear away the close entangled brambles, so that they might proceed at least without pain if without pleasure; and though the work was hard and made my hands bleed, and the good I effected was not great, I fancied I heard fewer groans, and I certainly felt less miserable myself. And now I made the invaluable discovery of an axe, strong and sharp, with which I cut away the hanging branches in all directions.

"My followers had certainly now a much clearer path before them; and as I rested for a moment from my labours, I listened for words of thanks and praise from them, but I was only greeted with ironical cheers and cries of 'If I had your axe, and your strength, I should not be contented with lopping a few miserable boughs, but whole trees should lie prostrate, and you should all breathe the fresh air, and see the pure light of day.'

"Angry and disheartened, I was half inclined to throw away my axe and give up such thankless work, but, fortunately for me, I received a wholesome rebuke from a poor little glow-worm which had been rudely thrust away by one of my fellow-travellers, with the angry exclamation of 'Begone, foolish insect, what use is your dim lamp; it only makes our darkness more dreary by reminding us of the light we have lost.' But the glow-worm returned to its path, and continued to give its feeble light — mocked and laughed at by some, thanked by a few, and useful in its little way to all.

"Shamed by the poor little glow-worm's example, I went on hacking away with all my strength at the thick ivy-grown branches, and at last I actually succeeded in making a gap through which a ray of light descended like a messenger of hope, and it shone upon a heap of those gems," continued he, pointing to the word "Love" on his casket, "and I took up some, and placed them there to carry to our King.

"When at last I came out of that deep forest I felt very happy, but I resolved, wherever I might be, to work for my poor fellow-travellers; and I always found something to do—now throwing away sharp stones from a rugged path, now planting upon some unsheltered common a little seedling, which, if watered with heaven's dew, may grow into a goodly tree, and give shade and pleasure to some future pilgrim.

"We cannot," continued Learsi, "disperse the clouds that often throw their dark shadow over us, nor have we power to stay the whirlwind, the icy blast, and the raging torrent, but we may do much to adorn our island and to smooth our fellow-travellers' way; and in doing so we shall be doubly blest,—we shall find the jewels for which our King has sent us hither, and, when we meet our fellow-travellers beyond the ocean, we shall meet in love those for whom we spent love and care on our journey here."

"Would that I might also work for my fellow-travellers," exclaimed Felicia; "but what can I do? I can only benefit them as a warning not to waste their time and energies in culling flowers which, at best, must wither and die. How can these hands, which have been only used to weave garlands, wield an axe, or even uproot one of those strong brambles?" and she raised her small thin hands before Learsi.

"We are not all called upon to cut down trees, nor to tear up brambles," he replied; " our strength, our opportunities, our very paths are different, and different also must be our labour; but never will an earnest will remain unsatisfied. When you were walking in that luxuriant meadow, might you not have gathered some of its flowers, not to adorn yourself, but to transplant to some less favoured spot, where they would have cheered the lonely traveller with their beauty and fragrance? Then you would not have felt the weariness of satiety, nor would your casket have been stained by the profusion of blossoms which you heaped upon it."

" Alas! alas!" exclaimed Felicia, " what might I not have done? Would that I could return, and make a better use of those scattered flowers!"

" To return is impossible," said Learsi; " but the withered blossoms need not be wholly lost; let them live in your memory, and they will not have bloomed or died in vain."

Though the travellers continued to walk and converse together, I could not hear their further discourse; but I perceived that Felicia listened with almost reverential attention to the words of her companion, and often tried to imitate his actions. Sometimes she would pick up weeds which were trailing on the path; sometimes she lent her little strength to his greater power to remove a heavy mass of stone, and repeatedly would she copy upon a leaf, or trace upon the sand, the words engraved in her casket, in order, I imagined, that any poor traveller whose casket, like hers, had once been dim and soiled, might find some comfort in his path, and directions for the discovery of jewels.

But now there are tears in Felicia's eyes, and Learsi, too, looks sad, and they seem to be bid-

ding each other adieu. The sound of Felicia's
voice died away before it reached me, but I understood the import of those unheard words; I
saw anguish written on that pale face; and I felt
that the greatest of all trials was now rending
that poor heart; she must part from her guide
and protector, and without love or sympathy toil
on alone to the end of her journey.

"Grieve not so deeply," urged Learsi, "but let
us be more diligent than ever in the search of
jewels, for the way is short, and we shall soon
hear the ocean's roar; and, dear Felicia," he
added, "once crossed the golden arch, we shall
meet again in a land far more blest than this
island; for has not our King told us that at His
right hand are pleasures for evermore? Remember," he continued, as she bowed her head with
the grief that would not be subdued, "remember
that sorrow endureth for a night, but joy cometh
in the morning." And as Learsi disappeared my
eyes seemed to become dim, I could distinguish
nothing distinctly, and I tried in vain to follow
Felicia's shadowy form. I could, however, still
discern her casket glittering through the hazy
atmosphere; and every now and then a new gem
gleamed upon it, like the stars in the twilight

hour, which greet us one by one with their radiant glances.

At last, however, I lost sight even of the casket. The hills and trees seemed to melt into air, the travellers became cloudlets, and the land began to undulate like the surrounding water. In another moment the Island of Jewels had vanished, but it left a track of gold and fire, as though a band of rubies was glittering under the transparent ocean. The sun was setting in all its fantastic glory, a monarch wrapped in his purple mantle, illuminating earth and sky with lights of every hue, which shone a bright farewell, and then expired as he departed.

The fresh breeze and sober grey which surrounded all those magical tints warned me that it was also time for me to depart, and to return to the realities and duties of home. Unlike the bright hour at which I had left my room, now all wore the dark monotonous livery of evening ; the gay flowers of my garden were almost concealed under the deep shadows of their foliage ; and my white cottage, peeping out through its dark screen of trees, looked like the ghost of its former self from its cypress churchyard. But, fortunately, I was also changed since the morning, and my heart was now full of peace and content, and yet I returned to the very same vexations and disappointments which had saddened me a few hours ago : care and sorrow had not vanished from the face of the world since noon, poverty and sickness were still around me ; what made me, then, feel so blithe and cheerful now ? Was it that the Island of Jewels had taught me an old but too often forgotten lesson, that we are not sent here to bask in the sunshine of happiness, no, nor even to seek it, but to toil after and win those precious gems, Faith, Love, Charity, Truth, Courage, and Fortitude, which can hardly be discovered in the noonday of prosperity, but which gleam upon us from the dark night of sickness and of sorrow ? I no longer thought myself like a poor flower planted in an adverse soil, which might have flourished in a more genial one, for I felt that wherever these jewels might be found there was a post of honour ; that a glorious task was before me, which required all my energy and strength ; and that mercy and righteousness ruled our destiny here, though we are often too blind to see, or too ignorant to recognise, the heavenly messengers sent to lead us to our God.

Woodfall and Kinder, Printers, Angel Court, Skinner Street, London.

For EU product safety concerns, contact us at Calle de José Abascal, 56–1°,
28003 Madrid, Spain or eugpsr@cambridge.org.

www.ingramcontent.com/pod-product-compliance
Ingram Content Group UK Ltd.
Pitfield, Milton Keynes, MK11 3LW, UK
UKHW012347130625
459647UK00009B/611

* 9 7 8 1 1 0 8 0 2 0 3 6 7 *